MW01234555

The
SEO
Entrepreneur

Start a Successful SEO Business and Turn Your Entrepreneurial Dreams Into Reality

NATHAN GOTCH

with Contributions from Simon L. Smith

DISCLAIMER

The publisher and author are not responsible for any actions you take or do not take as a result of reading this book, and are not liable for any damages or negative consequences from action or inaction to any person reading or following the information in this book. References are provided for informational purposes only and do not constitute endorsement of any websites or other sources. Readers should also be aware that the websites listed in this book may change or become obsolete.

CONTENTS

PART ONE:

A Business Model That Works for 99% of People

"The future depends on what you do today." -
Mahatma Gandhi

It's a million-dollar question.

What's the best way to get your feet wet with entrepreneurship? You might think the answer is to do something new or revolutionary.

It's not.

Instead, to increase your odds of success, you should use a proven business model. A model that's allowed me – an average guy – to build a wildly profitable business from the comfort of my home and achieve true financial success.

I didn't create the next Facebook or invent Bitcoin.

All I did was follow a tried-and-true business model that focuses on attracting the one thing that businesses care about more than anything else: more customers.

Because **if you know how to get more customers, you'll have one of the most valuable skills in the marketplace.** And search engine optimization (SEO) is the perfect vehicle for achieving that goal.

So back in 2013, I founded Gotch SEO with one mission in mind: to help as many businesses as I can achieve SEO success.

I then pursued that goal by packing my stuff up and driving from California to St. Louis.

I had no clients, no prospects, and no money (except for a credit card with a $500 limit).

I was also $40,000 in debt because of student and car loans.

Honestly, I was terrified and had every possible limiting belief enter my mind during that 27-hour drive...

"What if I fail?"... "What will people think about me?"

I could have crumbled from a case of "what ifs", but I pushed through it.

And guess what?

I landed my first several SEO clients within 30 days of moving to St. Louis.

I then grew Gotch SEO to six figures (profit) in less than 6 months and my life was never the same.

I'm not telling you this stuff to brag.

In fact:

I'm a very introverted and private person (ask my wife). I literally had knots in my stomach deciding whether or not to share the stuff above with you.

Here's the truth:

I wanted to share these things because I'm no different than you are. I was raised by a single mother in a low-income household. We actually lived in a trailer park at one point.

I also got horrible grades in school...

...and nearly got kicked out of college for my poor writing skills.

I sometimes go through funks and question everything I'm doing.

And I still, to this day, make TONS of mistakes in my business.

Why am I telling you all this?

Because if I can learn SEO, get real results, and grow hundreds of companies, then **there's nothing stopping you from doing the same.**

The truth is, learning how to drive consistent SEO results changed my life and my family's lives forever.

But here's the deal: learning SEO and understanding how to get results is a full-time job. A job that the average small business owner has no time to do. And that's when you come into play.

Believe it or not, businesses will pay you $1,000 - $10,000+ per month to help them get more customers through Google using SEO. I'm living proof of that fact.

That way, they don't have to try to figure it out themselves, and they can focus on what they're good at in their business. And you can make serious bank focusing on what you're good at – SEO. It's a win-win.

Speaking of which:

In this book, I'll show you how to build an incredibly profitable SEO business from A-Z using my proprietary "Lean Agency System."

Now let's get into it.

From SEO Zero to SEO Hero

"Once you make a decision, the universe conspires to make it happen." - Ralph Waldo Emerson

Make no mistake about it, discovering SEO changed my life.

But it wasn't all rainbows and lollipops, so let's rewind the clock back to 2011 before I started my client SEO agency.

I was on the path to becoming a lawyer, but I secretly wanted to build an online business. That way, I could work from anywhere and be my own boss. So, I spent my junior and senior years of college trying pointless things to make money online.

I did paid surveys. I sold random books on Amazon. I even wrote articles on article directories. But I was making pennies and knew it wouldn't work long-term.

Sound familiar?

But everything changed for me when I discovered a course called Web Colleagues. It had several techniques for making money online, but one stood out to me: blogging.

So I decided to start a blog about the one thing I had any experience in, which was baseball pitching. The name was

The Ultimate Pitcher – super creative, I know.

I spent months writing content and tweaking my blog design, and to no surprise, my blog was a ghost town.

That's when I went back to Google and searched "how to get traffic to my blog." There were all kinds of techniques, but SEO was the most intriguing to me. The idea that I could get free traffic from Google was revolutionary, and I went all in.

Long story short, I started implementing the various SEO tactics I learned – and to my amazement, they worked!

And then it happened.

My first affiliate commission was a whopping $47 in the winter of 2011. That $47 was all it took to go all-in on this idea of building an online business.

But here's where it gets interesting.

While I loved writing about baseball pitching, I realized that

SEO had become my true obsession. That's why I decided to test my SEO skills in other niches like fitness and under-the-counter ice makers. The weirdest part is that I wasn't creating these sites to make money. Instead, I was doing it to refine my SEO skills.

Truth be told, I saw SEO as my path to financial freedom and wanted to do whatever it took to be the best.

When I graduated college in 2012, I had several SEO projects going at once. But I wasn't earning enough to go out on my own yet, so I had to take on all kinds of oddball security jobs.

But although my time was extremely limited, every free moment I had was spent working on my SEO business.

I would wake up at 4:30 a.m. and work on my SEO projects before going to my day job at 9:00 a.m. I would also work on SEO during lunch and then do another night session after work.

I repeated this routine for over a year until something incredible happened: I got laid off.

So, I had two choices: find another nine-to-five job in Los Angeles or pack up my stuff and drive to St. Louis to be with my future wife. I chose the latter.

I then applied for every single SEO position in St. Louis. And guess what? I only got one measly response but did manage to land an interview. (Spoiler alert, I didn't get the job.)

Like most totally sane people would do, I decided to take matters into my own hands and try to get SEO clients on my own. My only goal was to make three thousand dollars a month because that was all I needed to survive.

But then something unexpected happened.

I hit that goal in less than thirty days. Then I hit ten thousand dollars a month soon after. Within a year, I hit thirty thousand dollars a month. And now, my SEO company has earned millions of dollars from client SEO services, training programs, and affiliate marketing.

Once again, I'm not trying to show off but just showing you what's possible if you apply yourself in the most lucrative industry online.

Want to know the best part?

You don't need to be a genius to do SEO. I got a 2.6 GPA in college and had zero prior entrepreneurship, business, or sales experience when I started.

Remember my first blog, The Ultimate Pitcher? What I didn't

tell you was that I accidentally misspelled "ultimate" when buying the domain name and actually purchased www. TheUlitmatePitcher.com.

The worst part was that I didn't even notice the mistake for six whole months while I built my blog on the wrong domain.

What's my point?

If someone like me can achieve this level of success, you absolutely can do the same and more.

So, follow my lead, be willing to fail, and become addicted to taking action. Let's do this!

Chapter 1:
The SEO Opportunity

"Decide what you want, and then act as if it were impossible to fail." – Brian Tracy

Good news:

There's never been a better time to enter the SEO industry.

While most people flock to social media or the latest fad in technology, SEO continues to be the most popular marketing channel for businesses. It's also exploding in growth and needs people who want to do great work.

But before I show you the proof, here's a question:

Did you know that three industries have created more millionaires than any other industry?

They are:
- Financial Services
- Technology
- Real estate

SEO falls under the *technology* category:

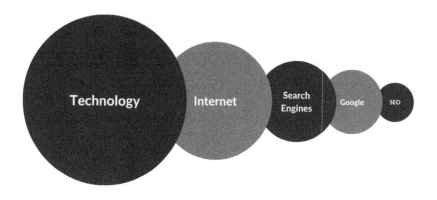

But that's not all because the SEO services market will grow beyond $134 billion by 2026 at a CAGR of 20.7% (Globe Newswire, 2022). To put that in perspective, huge industries like healthcare and construction have 11-12% annual growth. SEO is growing at a much more rapid rate (Forbes, 2022).

You can also go to the most popular freelancing platform, Upwork, to see how active the SEO industry is. At any given moment, there are thousands of SEO jobs available on Upwork. These are actual businesses looking for SEO help. All you need to do is apply for these opportunities to get clients.

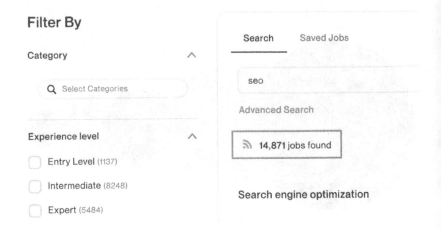

There are also over twelve thousand in-house SEO jobs available right now:

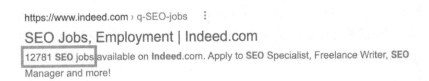

The point is that businesses need SEO help. There is massive demand and a low supply of SEO experts who can drive results. If you can deliver consistent SEO results, you'll get paid well.

In fact, according to a study by Ahrefs, most professionals charge between $1,000 - $5,000 per month for SEO services.

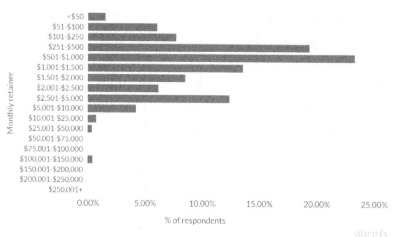

How Much Do SEOs Charge Per Month?

Imagine getting paid $1,000 per month to do SEO for a business. Multiply $1,000 x 10 businesses, and that's $10,000 per month offering SEO services.

Now here's the funny part:

That's actually a small retainer. My agency has a minimum retainer of $5,000 per month for national SEO campaigns.

How much you should charge will be based on your experience. But we'll talk about pricing later on.

The question is, why are businesses willing to invest so much money into SEO?

Why Businesses Love SEO

SEO isn't new. In fact, search engine optimization has been around since the late 1990s.

But it's still the most popular digital marketing channel. Surprisingly enough, it has more interest than social media marketing and Facebook ads combined.

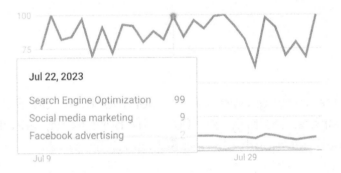

But there's a more powerful reason why businesses love SEO: intent.

Unlike social media, you know what someone is looking for when they search on Google. Based on their search query, you can deliver a page that serves them with one hundred percent relevance. As a result, conversion rates from search are far superior to any other channel.

That's not all. Organic social media marketing is also the ultimate hamster wheel. You get some awareness when you're posting, but when you stop, it's over.

SEO is different. SEO improves with time as long as you have a solid strategy in place.

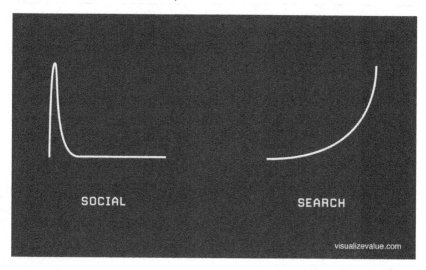

Case in point:

I have SEO-driven pages on gotchseo.com that have ranked in the top three on Google since 2015. I haven't touched these pages, but they still send free organic traffic and leads years later.

Remember that the more competitive the keyword, the more you'll have to work to keep it fresh. But the point is that SEO (once it's rolling) is not an endless hamster wheel. It can drive organic traffic, leads, and sales 24/7.

You might be wondering, is it too late to enter the SEO industry?

> *"The best time to plant a tree was twenty years ago.*
> *The second best time is now." - Chinese Proverb*

You might think you're too late to enter the SEO industry. But don't worry; there's tons of data proving otherwise.

First, despite SEO being around for a while, 57% of businesses do not have an SEO strategy, according to a recent survey of six hundred U.S. and Canadian small to medium-sized business owners (Search Engine Journal, 2022).

Second, only 30% of businesses would recommend their current SEO provider to a friend or colleague (Backlinko, 2022).

But there's more.

According to Ahrefs, **90.63% of web pages get 0 organic search traffic from Google** (Ahrefs, 2020).

So, the good news is that the bar is low because most SEO service providers are mediocre. I'll show you how to build an SEO service that stands out later.

Hint: it has to do with the root of the word SERVE.

Now that you know the SEO opportunity, let's discuss why you should focus on client SEO.

Chapter 2:
Why Client SEO is the Best Business Model

"There's no shortage of remarkable ideas; what's missing is the will to execute them." – Seth Godin

Let me say this straight, client SEO is the best business model for new entrepreneurs.

Here's why:

1. Cash Flow

The most significant benefit of client SEO is cash flow. You get paid upfront to deliver SEO services every single month. You can rely on this cash flow to build your business and invest in other revenue sources. Like the old saying goes, cash is king.

2. Low Barrier to Entry

You don't need years of experience or a huge budget to get started with client SEO. All you need is a willingness to learn a new skill set. To put it in perspective, I started my SEO business with a credit card that had a five-hundred-dollar limit. I used sweat equity to build everything else.

3. You're the Boss

You control when you work, who you work with, and how much you get paid. That makes you the boss of your business. And your job is to serve your clients and deliver positive outcomes. That's why they're paying you. But unlike a traditional job, you don't have to put up with anyone you don't vibe with and you can fire your nightmare clients whenever you wish. I've done it more times than I can count, which leads to the next benefit.

4. Freedom

Besides the freedom of working with clients you like, you can decide when, where, and how you build your daily schedule. Want to sleep in because you're a night owl and prefer to work late? No problem. Or perhaps you're an early bird and would like to get most of your work done before noon. It's all possible. Also, you can work from anywhere – home, coffee shops, wherever you prefer, – all you need is a laptop and WiFi connection. The choices are endless.

5. Zero Income Ceiling

Most regular jobs have an income ceiling. Client SEO does not. There is no limit to how much money you can earn because you get paid for results, not by the hour. But keep in mind that it's not a straight line. You will face hurdles at each level of revenue you reach. For example, at $20,000/ month (nearly $250k/year), you may want to start hiring virtual assistants to delegate some of the SEO work to. That's good – because now you have an opportunity to start working less in your business so you can invest more time working on your business to enter the next tier of revenue. Don't worry; keep reading and I'll show you exactly how to surpass the most common plateaus you'll encounter.

The Paths

"You cannot make progress without making decisions." — Jim Rohn

Look, no matter what your situation is right now, there's a path to getting started with client SEO. If you have the will, there's always a way.

Here are a few options to consider:

1. Keep Your Day Job

Many people glamorize this idea of "going all in" or "burning the boats." While it does have merit, it's not the best idea for most people. You can keep your day job and use some of your income to fund your SEO business. As a result, it reduces your risk.

Now I will say this: You can alter this method based on what stage of life you're in. You can be riskier if you're super young, single, don't have kids, and have very few obligations (like a mortgage or college savings). Burning the boats is a solid strategy when you're young because you don't have a lot to lose.

Otherwise, use sweat equity until you replace your current income.

For example, if you earn $100,000/year at your day job, then all you need to do is get to $8,333/month with client SEO. That can happen in less than six months if you're motivated.

How do I know? Because that's what happened to me.

I earned over $104,000 in profit in my first year of doing client SEO. But I had no clue what I was doing. The good news is you'll be lightyears ahead of where I was because of this framework I'm giving you.

2. Start with an Affiliate Website

Listen, take every SEO client you can get in the beginning. But it's easier to get clients with a portfolio.

So how do you handle this catch-22? Simple. Get results with a website you own. In other words, you are the client.

If you want to go that route, find a niche you're interested in and build a content-rich website. Keep your focus on very low-competition keywords.

And here's the cool part: every keyword you rank for becomes an asset to your portfolio.

You can then leverage your results to earn client SEO business. More on this later.

3. See How They Make the Sausage

This one might shock you, but something you need to consider is getting hired by an SEO agency.

Here's why:

You'll Get to Build Your Portfolio (Fast)

The agency's clients are your clients. So, if you're responsible for the results, you can use the results to build your own portfolio.

You'll Get Experience

Working within an agency is an amazing way to accelerate your experience by encountering many unique SEO scenarios. Nothing else will prepare you better for solo client SEO work.

You'll See How Successful Agencies Operate

There is no faster way to learn the business side of running an SEO agency than by watching someone else do it well. So, watch, learn, and take notes. These invaluable lessons will help you when you venture out on your own.

Pick Your Path

Don't overthink this part. You can use a combination of the strategies I've mentioned above or put together your own. Either way, you need experience, and your SEO portfolio needs to grow. Your portfolio is critical to successful client acquisition, so do everything you can start building it now.

Chapter 3:
How to Think (Like a Successful SEO Entrepreneur)

"Your life today is a result of your thinking yesterday. Your life tomorrow will be determined by what you think today." — John C. Maxwell

Breaking news: the wrong mindset will stop you from being successful.

The great Tony Robbins often says that success is 80% psychology and 20% mechanics. And it's 100% true.

I know this from my own experience.

I grew up with terrible thinking models and didn't realize how bad they were until I read my first book after college.

The book was called *Psycho-Cybernetics* and it changed my life by teaching me how to view the world and think about success. After that, I was hooked and read hundreds of psychology, personal development, and business books.

But nothing taught me more about the importance of your mindset than going through the school of hard knocks and running my own SEO business for ten years.

Here's the deal:

If you want to live a 1% life, you have to think like the 1%. You have to view things differently than the 99%. And most importantly, you have to act in a completely different way than most folks.

You must become a wolf instead of a sheep.

But don't worry, there's nothing shady or negative about the following mindsets you need to adopt if you want to be successful:

Everything Is Your Fault

Take a minute and think about someone you know personally who has a victim-mentality and always blames everything in their life on someone or something else: the government, society, their boss, spouse, friends, parents, the list goes on.

Now ask yourself how successful are they?

This is why you must take one hundred percent responsibility for everything in your business (and life). It's easy to point fingers and deflect blame when things don't go your way. And it's hard to accept that you're responsible – even when it doesn't seem like you are.

But if you want to end average thinking, it starts with this simple mindset shift. When you take full responsibility, it opens the door to vastly more opportunities.

Instead of deflecting and saying, *"It's so-and-so's fault,"* you should say, *"In some way, this is my fault. I'll find where I made a mistake and work to fix it."* See the difference?

Now I know you might be thinking, "What about situations where you literally have no fault whatsoever, like a business partner steals from you or someone rear-ends you with their car?"

Fair question but don't take this concept so literally that you miss the point:

When you play the victim, you do nothing to correct the problem except pass the buck. But when you accept responsibility, you immediately start looking for solutions.

And the truth is that most problems stem from poor systems, not people. That's why you need to adopt a systems-dependent mindset.

So instead of blaming an individual, you need to reflect on the system that guides them. Ask, *"What's broken in this process that led to the poor outcome?"* We'll get into this later.

Eliminate Incongruent Thinking

Question:

How can you ask a business to invest thousands of dollars into your professional SEO business if you haven't invested a single dime into becoming a professional?

That's incongruent and it will affect you on a subconscious level.

The infamous MMA fighter Conor McGregor learned this lesson from another athlete:

"I read something about LeBron James a while back about maybe a year ago," McGregor said. "That he spent $1.5 million annually on his health, himself. His everything. His nutritionists, trainers, everything. And I spent nothing. Only in training camp."

With LeBron in mind, McGregor realized he had spent a fortune on material things while not investing in his body.

"I drop money on a bleeding car, or a watch," McGregor said. "So I'm like, spend it on myself. My health, my fitness, and that's helped me. And then you're going to acquire even more when you're sharp, and that's what I am now."

I'm not suggesting you need to run out and hire a nutritionist like a pro athlete, but hopefully you get the point about self-improvement if you're an aspiring entrepreneur.

It's deceptively simple, but you need to invest in yourself and your business if you expect someone to invest their hard-earned dollars into your SEO services. That's why I increase my business and personal education investment every year.

If you do that, you'll have conviction and confidence when you sell your services. Why? Because you'll practice what you preach.

Think "Investment," Not Cost

Never say this to an SEO prospect: "It'll cost $1,000/month."

SEO is not a "cost." It's an investment.

For every one dollar you put in, you're hoping to get two dollars (or more) back. It's not like buying a TV that depreciates. You need to know the difference to be successful in entrepreneurship.

For example, if I said I could help you make over $100,000 by starting an SEO business, would you invest $10,000?

Your answer to this question will determine a lot about your current thinking.

If you said, *"heck yes, that's an awesome deal,"* then you're thinking the right way. But, on the other hand, if you said, *"Woah... I don't have ten thousand dollars. Are you insane?"* then you're thinking about it the wrong way.

Money is a renewable resource. And there's an unlimited supply if you know how to get it.

The second thinker is living in the confines of a scarcity mindset. That person views everything as a cost, not an investment.

You cannot sell SEO services to a business if you think this way. You must believe that your SEO services will generate a return on your investment (ROI). And you must sell the services based on the potential ROI.

But, again, this goes back to incongruent thinking. If you want your prospects to view your SEO solution as an investment, you must think the same way.

But thinking isn't enough. You must also reflect this idea through your behavior.

How to Create Goals (That Actually Work)

"The trouble with not having a goal is that you can spend your life running up and down the field and never score." – Bill Copeland

Disclaimer: I promise this won't be self-help nonsense. Every recommendation I'm about to give you relies on research and data. In other words, it works!

According to Harvard, 83% of the population don't have goals but the 17% who have goals are ten times more successful than those without goals.

Of the goal-setters, they also found that only 3% have goals written down. But get this: the 3% with written goals are three times more successful than the 14% with unwritten goals (Harvard, 2015).

There are two obvious points to pull from this data: First, you need goals, and second, you need to write them down.

So if you want to be ten times more successful, here's how to create goals (the right way):

Lead vs. Lag Goals

There are two types of goals: leading and lagging.

Lagging goals are what most people understand and time to achieve. You create a goal like *"lose ten pounds."* It's a lagging outcome and whether you get there or not is dependent on your lead goals.

Leading goals are the actions that will produce the outcome you want in the future. For weight loss, a lead goal could be *"I will walk 3 miles every day this week."*

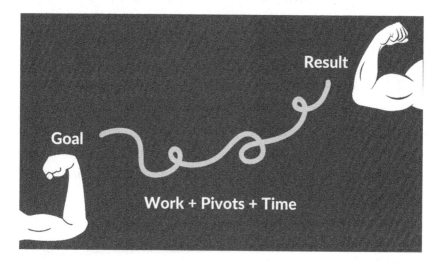

Bottom line is lagging goals without practical steps to achieve them – leading goals – are just dreams. It's not proactive.

The only way you can achieve your goals is to work backward. What are the core actions you need to take to accomplish the goal? What does that look like monthly, weekly, and daily? Break it down into tiny, super-achievable steps.

It's obvious why you need leading goals, but why do you need lagging goals? Reframe the idea into a different context. Think about traveling somewhere.

For example, imagine you wanted to visit the ancient ruins known as Machu Picchu in Peru.

Now that you have a specific destination (lagging goal), you can start planning on flights, accommodations, backpacking guides, etc. (leading goals) that will be required to get there.

Make sense?

So having a lagging target allows you to work backward and plan a realistic roadmap. Like the late Zig Ziglar said, *"You can't hit a target you cannot see, and you cannot see a target you do not have."*

But how do you set an effective target or goal in the first place? Glad you asked.

SMART Goals

This simple framework will help you create goals that produce results.

"SMART" stands for Specific, Measurable, Attainable, Relevant, and Time-Bound.

To begin, here's an example of poor goal-setting:

"I want more SEO clients."

This goal isn't specific – how many clients? It isn't measurable; it needs a quantifiable number. We don't know whether it's attainable because there's no target and no deadline attached. Also, notice the phrasing of the goal – "I want…" Weak language and lack of conviction produces poor outcomes.

Here's a better example using the SMART formula:

"I will easily close ten new SEO clients by December 1st."

Notice the difference? This goal has conviction, is specific, measurable, attainable, relevant, and has a deadline.

Remember, this is only the first stage of the goal-setting process. Now that you have your lag goal, you must establish your lead goals.

Use the same SMART framework for each leading goal such as:

- "I will submit one SEO proposal on Upwork every day."

- "I will reach out to one business who needs SEO help in my local area every day."

These leading goals hit each part of the framework, but I want you to focus on one thing:

See how "attainable" I've made the goals?

Don't set lofty, pie in the sky, unachievable goals. Consistent daily action will produce much better outcomes. And once you've hit your daily targets for at least thirty days, consider upping them.

Check this out:

I heard a story told by serial entrepreneur Tim Ferriss dating back to when IBM was the dominant force in their industry. At the time, IBM was well-known for having one of the most effective sales teams in the world.

So, what did they do differently?

Instead of having impossible sales quotas, they set super small targets. The rationale was that they didn't want their salespeople to be intimidated to pick up the phone. As a result, it would build sales momentum – and people would actually **overshoot** their goals (Tim Ferriss on Goal Setting: Rig the Game so You Can Win It, 2016).

The point is that small, achievable goals are more effective since nothing is more motivating than seeing progress and slowly but surely moving closer to your bigger goal.

Pop quiz: What are one to three goals you want to achieve with your SEO business this year?

Write them down, keep them in a visible location, and review them daily to stay on track. I highly recommend using a tool such as The Five Minute Journal (Google it) which is a great way to set and review your targets on a daily basis.

Trust me on this: Creating SMART goals will put you ahead of most people. Writing them down and reviewing them on a regular basis will make you unstoppable.

However, you should consider adding two final strategies to make your success much more predictable.

Accountability

"Give vulnerability a shot. Give discomfort its due. A person's success in life can usually be measured by the number of uncomfortable conversations he or she is willing to have." – Tim Ferriss

A recent study from the Association for Talent Development found that people who decide to do something on their own – no plan – have about a 25% chance of accomplishing it.

But get this: People who commit to someone (like a trainer or coach) improve their odds of success to around 65%.

Crazy, right?

But the study takes it even further: If you schedule the actions and are accountable, your success rate climbs to 95%.

So, what's the takeaway from this study?

First, you need an effective goal structure, which you now have. Second, you need accountability. In other words, you need someone to report to and someone who can check on your progress.

You might be thinking, *"Hold on, I thought I was an*

entrepreneur and didn't need other people!"

Big mistake. Solo entrepreneurs (without any employees) have this mentality. It's fine in the beginning. You can get decent success as a solo artist.

But to get to the next level, you'll need help.

Otherwise, you'll have to work sixteen-hour days for the rest of your life. And that's not a business. That's a job.

A real business is a living entity that operates and grows without you.

But here's the takeaway: **You need an accountability partner**.

Think about it. Who can you meet up with weekly to discuss your progress?

I don't recommend friends or family. Instead, you need someone who can give you some tough love. But, of course, the best person is someone who has already achieved the goals you want.

I recommend joining some communities and building relationships. You can find someone at your level or a little higher than you. Then, you can set up a weekly accountability meeting. You can also try a service like Stickk.com.

The data supports having accountability, but I'll tell you from my own personal experience.

When I started having weekly meetings with accountability partners, my revenue doubled. I even crushed the plateaus I was stuck at for years.

It's the most impactful thing I've ever done in my business. Everyone – even self-motivated people – can benefit from accountability.

Now you might be wondering, what are you reporting in these accountability meetings?

The most important things to discuss are what you've done and what's next.

Remember: Results are a lagging indicator. It's the leading goals (actions) that lead to results. Focus on the actions.

At this point, you know how to create effective goals – and hopefully you can find someone to hold you accountable.

Now let's add the last piece of the puzzle.

Vision Board

I know, I know – for some of you this may sound like motivational woo-woo but let me put it this way:

A recent study shows that 1 in 5 successful entrepreneurs use vision boards (Inc, 2022). So why not give yourself every advantage possible for success?

Most people are visual learners and when something is out of sight, it's out of mind. Especially when it comes to your goals

Many people write their goals down, which is effective. And it's already better than the vast majority of folks who have no goals whatsoever. But you also need to create a vision (or visual) of the achieved goal.

For example, I have a picture of our home on my vision board. It reminds me that I want to own our home by paying off the mortgage early. I also have images of leaders, athletes, motivational words, and other objects that inspire me to keep working towards my goals.

So, I have them all written down – and I see them every day. You can use a free tool like Canva.com to create your own vision board with their easy-to-use templates.

Then go to Google, grab images that best represent your goals, and put them together. Most importantly, print it out and place your vision board somewhere that allows you to look at it every single day.

And there you have it.

Now do yourself a favor and re-read this entire chapter on goal-setting. If you take action on the strategies outlined above, I guarantee you'll see significant improvements in your life and success.

PART TWO:

The Foundation

"Someday is not a day of the week." – Denise Brennan-Nelson

Fact: How you structure your SEO business today will determine how valuable it is tomorrow.

Do not take this section lightly! Take your time and think deeply about each of these concepts so you start off on the right foot.

Let's start with the most critical question:

Chapter 4:
What is the "Lean Agency System"?

The "Lean Agency System" is built for time freedom and maximum profitability.

The truth is that most agency owners are burned out and making very little money compared to how much time they're investing in their company.

But you don't need to work sixteen hours a day to build a successful SEO business. You simply need the right blueprint to follow.

So instead of hiring a bunch of people, you're going to focus on building a team around your systems. Systems lead the way. People operate within those systems.

Think about any successful sports team like the Chicago Bulls or Los Angeles Lakers when Phil Jackson was the head coach. These basketball teams were filled with talented players like Michael Jordan and Kobe Bryant, but they only won a championship once they operated within a system.

Phil Jackson's system was the triangle offense. Once the team embraced the system, they achieved tremendous success.

Similarly, you must become systems-dependent if you want to build a profitable SEO business from scratch.

The Lean Agency System has three parts:

1. Start

This phase aims to build a strong foundation and consists of Attack, Attract, and Close to help you land your first handful of clients.

Attack

You'll be on the offensive in this stage since you likely won't have any established inbound channels. So, you'll need to seek out clients instead of waiting for them to come to you.

Attract

You can build an entire business on the "Attack" methods. But if you want to scale, you must also learn how to attract leads and clients. They need to come to you through inbound marketing. I'll show you how to build inbound marketing channels that drive new leads and clients 24/7.

Close

The "Attack" and "Attract" stages are how you get relevant, high-quality leads. But you still have to turn those leads into clients. That's where the "Close" stage comes in. I'll show you my proven process for converting leads into loyal clients.

The goal is to reach $10,000 - $20,000/month. Most of this book will focus on getting you to $10,000/month with client SEO.

Once you hit it, it's time for phase two.

2. Systemize

You already have a nice pool of clients in this phase but are starting to feel the pain. In other words, the work is becoming overwhelming and unsustainable. Good problem to have.

That's when building systems become paramount to breaking through this plateau. Once you've built and tested your systems, it's time to build a team.

3. Scale

You can only go so far by yourself. To scale, you need both systems and a team. The good news is that you don't need to hire someone for $100,000/year. Instead, I'll show you exactly how to build a team in the most profitable way possible.

But here's the truth:

You shouldn't be thinking about systemization and scaling until you hit at least $10,000/month. Until then, 100 percent of your focus needs to be one hundred percent on client acquisition. And that's what I'm going to show you right now.

Chapter 5:
Pick a Niche

"The beauty of the Internet is there's a niche market for everything, and if you can focus on it, you can build a sustainable and viable business of it." – Michelle Phan

---

In my experience, niching down is the path of least resistance when you're new to the SEO game.

The reason is simple:

Instead of competing with established agencies, it becomes a competition of one. The goal is to become the "go-to" SEO expert in a small niche. You want to be a big fish in a small pond.

Think about it: Is it easier to become the go-to SEO expert for the entire US or the go-to SEO expert for endodontists?

There are thousands of SEO companies competing on the national and local levels. Most are not niche-targeted.

How many SEO companies focus on endodontists? I struggled to find even one on Google.

Here's the truth: You don't need a ton of clients to build a successful SEO business. You only need the right niche, and you need to focus. Here's how to do it.

Don't Be Picky (When You're New)

You should niche down, but you should also say YES to any opportunity that comes your way.

The goal at this point isn't to get rich overnight. The goal is to build a portfolio and get professional experience as fast as possible.

You'll then be able to leverage this portfolio which will make it easier to earn more business as you grow.

So, take what you can get in the beginning, but maintain the long-term idea of niching down. Also, by working with a variety of clients, you'll be able to see what niches you like or don't like.

That said, be aware that 90% of top SEO companies are not niche-targeted (Clutch, 2022).

You can view this in two different ways.

First, it's a sign that niching down could be an effective differentiation strategy for someone just getting started. Second, it's signaling that there's already a proven blueprint to follow.

In other words, keep in mind that these top SEO companies are well-established. So, if you're just starting out, it's wise to start small. For example, think about Amazon which began as a small online bookstore.

The truth is that big SEO companies are often complacent and slow. And in most cases, it's too difficult for them to shift their focus to a specific niche. Plus, they don't need to because they're already doing well. So, look at it as your opportunity.

Here are some techniques you can use to niche down:

Niche Method #1 - Industry

By far, the most common way to niche down is by choosing an industry to focus on.

For example, you can become the go-to SEO expert for immigration lawyers.

Then you can build your entire marketing and sales process around one ideal client. It also makes it easier to fulfill your SEO services because you'll know the niche better than anyone.

I find the best way to approach this strategy is to focus on industries with high customer value like the following niches:

Here are some niches with high customer values to consider:

Legal: Personal Injury, Criminal, Immigration, Family, Divorce, or Patent Lawyers.

Health: Hospitals, Dentists, Orthodontists, Periodontists, Prosthodontists, Endodontists, Pediatric Dentists, Cosmetic Dentists, Plastic Surgeons, or Eye Doctors.

Local: Jewelers, Architects, Property Managers, Real Estate, HVAC, Plumbers, Electricians, or Water Restoration.

B2B: Web Design, Video Production, Technology, or SaaS.

Note: These are just examples and by no means an exhaustive list of niches with high customer values that you can target.

Another idea is to check out a site like Angi.com and see if any niches catch your eye.

Top categories

Air Duct Cleaning	Hurricane Shutters
Animal Removal	HVAC Companies
Antenna Repair	Insulation
Appliance Repair	Interior Decorators
Architect	Interior Painting
Asbestos Removal	Iron Work

But what about real-life SEO companies?

One of the best examples in the SEO industry of niching down is Rankings.io.

Rankings.io focuses 100% on doing SEO for personal injury lawyers.

The only SEO agency for lawyers with a 94% retention rate

There's also plumberseo.net which started by only focusing on plumbers. Now they've expanded out to HVAC.

There are countless success stories like these companies. All you need to do is pick a niche and focus.

Niche Method #2 - Location

The second method is to niche down by location. For example, you can become the go-to SEO expert in Chicago. In this case, you're casting a wider net and will be working with many different industries.

If you're new, I don't recommend targeting a large metropolitan area.

Start with a surrounding city with a high net worth.

For example, when I started, I targeted Santa Monica and

Glendale instead of Los Angeles. I ranked for keywords like "Santa Monica SEO" and still rank to this day.

I did the same thing for "St Louis SEO" in 2014 and Gotch SEO still ranks today.

These geo-targeted pages still send me leads on autopilot.

I recommend building a focused site like santamonicaseopro. com instead of a bunch of landing pages. Then build the entire website around this one location. You'll be able to rank much easier because you'll have hyper-focused topical authority.

Niche Method #3 - Service

The third method is to splinter the larger SEO process into productized services. Instead of the "SEO guy," you can be the go-to link-building, on-page SEO, or keyword research specialist.

You might think you'll miss out on revenue by only offering one small service.

But here's where things get interesting.

You can offer these services (like keyword research) on the front end. Then, you can sell the larger SEO package on the backend once you've demonstrated that you do great work.

For example, Loganix offers micro-SEO services to SEO agencies.

logani✗   LOCAL SEO ⌄ SEO ⌄ PPC ⌄ CONTENT ⌄ LINK BUILDING ⌄ RESOURCES ⌄ ABOUT US CONTACT US LOGIN SIGN UP

Hand off the toughest tasks in
SEO, PPC, and content without
compromising quality

Scale and speed up delivery with the partner trusted by the pros.

So, if you want to serve business owners, this may not be the best option. It's also more of a project-based model.

That means you'll have to keep closing new clients and trying to attract recurring sales.

But on the flip side, with full-service SEO, you'll get paid every month from the same client.

That said, micro-SEO services function well as front-end offers, which I'll be covering soon.

Niche Method #4 - Niche + Service

The fourth method is to pick a service within the SEO process and then focus on a niche. For example, one of our Gotch SEO Academy members, Alan Silvestri, built a link building business for SaaS companies.

He's doing tremendously well because he has almost no competition. And when a SaaS company needs link building, they think of him. This strategy also leads to more referrals because now he's "the guy" for SaaS link building.

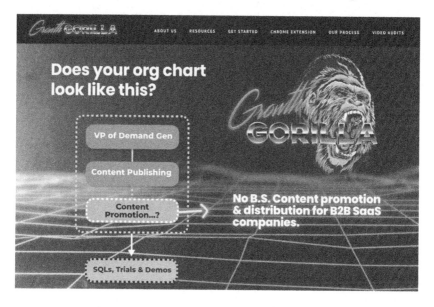

Once you're "the guy" for something, it becomes so much easier to scale your business.

Here's the kicker: Picking a niche is only the first step.

So stick with me here as I show you how to find angles for distinguishing yourself from the competition.

Become the Purple Cow

"In a crowded marketplace, fitting in is failing. In a busy marketplace, not standing out is the same as being invisible." – Seth Godin

---

Picture this:

Imagine that the SEO world is a pasture and every SEO company is a cow.

All the cows look the same, but now imagine looking out and seeing a purple cow. It would stop you because it's so different and abnormal.

That sums up the "Purple Cow" concept created by marketing genius Seth Godin. You don't want to "compete" with all the other cows. Instead, you want to focus on differentiation.

The question is, how? Here are some angles you can test to set yourself apart from the pack:

Angle #1 - YOU

I used to think that building a brand around a person was a bad bet. And this is coming from someone who named their brand after their last name, "Gotch SEO."

But come to find out, it's not a detriment at all. Many iconic brands like Disney, Baskin-Robbins, Cadillac, and others use their founders' names (Wikipedia, 2022):

A [edit]

- A. G. Edwards – Albert Gallatin Edwards
- A&M Records – Herb Alpert and Jerry Moss
- A&W Restaurants – Roy Allen and Frank Wright
- Abbott Laboratories – Wallace Calvin Abbott (1888)
- Abercrombie & Fitch – David T. Abercrombie and Ezra Fitch
- Abrams Air Craft – Talbert Abrams
- Abt Sportsline – Johann Abt
- Adam Opel AG – Adam Opel
- Adidas – Adi Dassler (Adolf Dassler)
- Aditya Birla Group – Ghanshyam Das Birla
- Agusta – Giovanni Agusta
- AGV – Gino Amisano (Amisano Gino Valenza)
- Air Jordan – Michael Jordan

Does this mean you should go this route? Not necessarily, but it's always an option. The truth is that a name isn't a brand. Names mean very little on their own. Your brand is what people think about when they hear your name.

But when it comes to differentiation, you're the best option because no one else is you.

And if you need more proof, look at one of the biggest

advertising agencies, Ogilvy. Ogilvy was founded by David Ogilvy, one of the greatest sales copywriters ever. Ogilvy is now a multi-billion-dollar company in large part because of what the Oglivy name represents to this day. (Zippia, 2022).

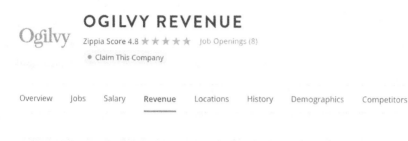

OGILVY REVENUE

Ogilvy   Zippia Score 4.8 ★ ★ ★ ★ ★   Job Openings (8)

● Claim This Company

Overview   Jobs   Salary   **Revenue**   Locations   History   Demographics   Competitors

Ogilvy's Annual Revenue
$5.9 Billion

But, once again, a name is just a name. It's what you do with it that matters. Don't forget that most people prefer to work with people over generic corporations. And it's a huge advantage when you're new because companies like to speak to the expert (not an intern).

Keep in mind that branding yourself may become a challenge down the road when you're trying to scale your company, but I call that a great problem to have. And when you're just starting out, the benefits of becoming the face or expert of your brand can be worth it – I'm living proof.

Angle #2 - Embrace Being Small

Authenticity is more important than ever and the worst thing you can do in the beginning is pretend to be bigger than you are.

In my experience, many companies know they'll get focused attention working with smaller agencies instead of being another number on a big agency's roster. Lean on the fact that you're small. It's a strength, not a weakness.

Angle #3 - Technology

Having some proprietary technology is a great way to differentiate yourself from the crowd. For example, WebFX has a suite of SEO tools that integrate with their SEO services. They stand out because they have a unique technological advantage over other agencies.

Angle #4 - Design

Design is another way to easily differentiate yourself. One of our members of Gotch SEO Academy, Alan Silvestri, executed this angle perfectly.

He uses an 80s retro design for his brand, Growth Gorilla. And he also loves *Back to the Future*. So, there are two easily identifiable characteristics of his brand.

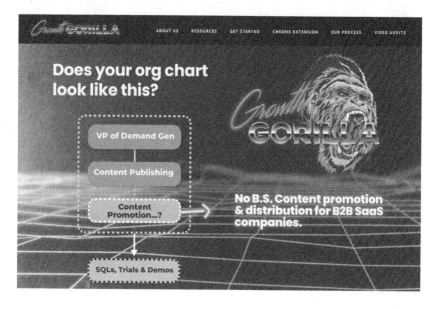

As I previously mentioned, he's also focusing on link building for B2B SaaS companies. Combined together, you can see why Alan is successfully doing what's required to differentiate himself in a crowded market.

Angle #5 - Productize

Webris is an SEO agency that does this exceptionally well by offering three types of "sprints."

So instead of pitching a monthly retainer, they pitch productized packages. We'll discuss using front-end offers to get clients in the door later.

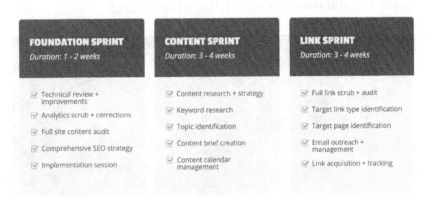

But for now, don't feel like monthly retainers are the only thing you can sell. You can slice the SEO process into smaller pieces and sell those as products.

As you can see, there are many ways to become the purple cow in your space. Don't overthink this concept. Just keep in mind that you should leverage all angles that make sense for your situation and you don't need to pick just one.

Establish a USP

"Fresh hot pizza, delivered in thirty minutes or less or it's free." - Domino's

---

A USP (Unique Selling Proposition) is the one thing that makes your business better than the competition. Here are some examples from other industries:

- *"The World's Strongest Coffee"* - Death Wish Coffee

- *"Payments infrastructure for the internet"* - Stripe

- *"Investing for everyone"* - Robinhood

- *"Fresh hot pizza, delivered in thirty minutes or less or it's free."* - Domino's

- *"Expect More. Pay Less."* - Target

- *"Plants made easy"* - Patch

I recommend this format for your SEO business:

"We help [NICHE] [RESULT] by [SOLUTION]."

Example #1:

"We help small businesses in Chesterfield get more organic traffic, leads, and sales through SEO."

Example #2:

"We help cyber security companies get ten times more leads and clients through SEO."

Notice how different the USP would be without picking a niche:

"We help companies get more organic traffic, leads, and sales through SEO."

The problem with being broad is that by trying to please everyone, you won't appeal to anyone. You want your positioning to catch your ideal client's attention. You want them to raise their hand and say, "That's *me!*" It's no secret that small and large companies alike want to work with those who they feel know their industry.

And the reason why I've hammered this idea of niching down is that most beginners won't do it. Most beginners think they must dominate the entire SEO industry to win clients. And that's a big mistake.

Chew on this for a second:

According to a 2019 study, there are 5,711 active endodontists in the US (Statista, 2019). If you become the go-to SEO expert for endodontists and get only 1% of the market, you'll have 57 clients. Even if you only charged $500/month, that's $28,555/month. At a $1,000/month rate, you're up to $57,000/month.

And that's only when you capture 1% of the market.

So the USP for endodontists could be as simple as: "We help endodontists get ten times more patients through SEO."

Notice that I used "patients" and not "customers." Always use the language of the target industry. For example, if you were targeting SaaS, you would talk about SQLs (Sales Qualified Leads) like Directive does so well:

Speaking in your target market's language is one of the best ways to show you understand their industry better than most.

Establish Your Brand Design

"Your brand is the single most important investment you can make in your business." - Steve Forbes

Listen, your brand's aesthetic and overall design can influence your prospects a ton. But don't overthink it in the beginning.

This is one area where people spend way too much time trying to figure out. They'll keep tweaking their design instead of focusing on higher-impact actions. Plus, you can always upgrade your design once you have consistent cash flow.

Here are a few key actions to take:

Pick A Brand Name

Once again, don't overthink this. Your brand name has no meaning on its own. Instead, your "brand" is how the market perceives what you do.

And that's why I spent very little time naming my SEO company.

Hence the creative name – Gotch SEO. And guess what?

People now associate my brand with giving tremendous value. It has nothing to do with my name and everything to do with the work I've put in over many years.

Spend no more than an hour picking your SEO company name.

Get A Domain

Once you've picked a brand name, you need to see if the domain name is available. While there are all kinds of fancy Top Level Domains (TLDs) these days, I still recommend getting .com. The only reason is familiarity.

People are familiar with .com TLDs versus something more modern like .agency.

Start by going to instantdomainsearch.com and see if your name is available. If not, you'll have to try some variations.

Once you've found an available domain, I recommend going with a fantastic web host known as SiteGround. You can get both your domain and hosting with SiteGround. Trust me, this makes things much more manageable.

Pick A Color Scheme

Every successful brand has a recognizable color scheme. Think about Coca-Cola, UPS, or even Pepsi. Next, I recommend going onto Canva and using their "Brand Kit" section to establish your colors.

You only need one primary color and two secondary colors. You'll use these colors on your website and your marketing materials.

One thing I recommend is to analyze your competitors. In general, your brand colors should contrast nicely with theirs. It doesn't have to be crazy, just different.

Create A Logo

Every brand needs a logo. But this is another point that will slow you down if you let it. There is no perfect logo, and it's also not critical to your success. Plus, you can always upgrade your logo later. There are a few ways to create a logo based on budget levels.

The first is to use Canva. Canva comes with logo templates that are sleek and customizable. The second option is to use Fiverr. You can get a decent logo from Fiverr for super cheap. And the final but most expensive option is to use a service like 99 Designs. You can run a logo design contest and then pick the one you like the most.

Create A Brand Email

You'll need a professional email address if you're serious about building trust. It's hard to trust sillystring213@gmail. com. Instead, you need joe@awesomeseocompany.com. The easiest way to get a business email is to use Google Workspace. Or if you use SiteGround for hosting, they also allow you to create branded emails for free.

Create Your Website

"Your website is the window of your business. Keep it fresh, keep it exciting." – Jay Conrad Levinson

Note: I'm going to mention a few themes and tools in this section that are working extremely well for me as of this writing. But as we all know, technology evolves and changes rapidly so what works today may not work tomorrow. Adapt. Improvise. Overcome.

At this point, you should have a domain and hosting. Now it's time to set your website up on what I feel is the best Content Management System (CMS), WordPress.

If you picked SiteGround, the process of installing WordPress is super simple.

Follow their instructions here: SiteGround.com/tutorials/wordpress/installation/

After WordPress is installed, you'll need to set up an SSL certificate.

Instructions are here: SiteGround.com/tutorials/getting-started/add-ssl-site/

Now you'll need to optimize some basic WordPress settings.

Set Up WordPress

Once you've logged into your website's WordPress dashboard, go to **Settings** and click on **General**. You'll need to decide if you want the "www." subdomain. There is no benefit either way, it's a matter of personal preference. If you do change it, make sure you change it on both the **WordPress Address (URL)** and **Site Address (URL)** fields.

You'll get logged out when you make this change. Log back in, and the change will be active.

Next, go to **Settings** and click on **Permalinks**. Select **Post name** as the URL structure.

This is the ideal structure for most websites. The main reason is that it allows you to update your pages without changing the URL structure. For example, with "Day and name," the URL structure looks like this:

https://www.gotchseo.com/2022/08/24/sample-post/

But if you update that post next month, it will be:

https://www.gotchseo.com/2022/09/24/sample-post/

As a result, the old post will require a 301 redirect (viewed as a permanent redirect by search engines) to the new post, which may leak authority.

Install WordPress Theme

GeneratePress is one of the best WordPress themes on the market today. It loads blazingly fast, super customizable, and very user-friendly. You can learn how to use it in a weekend; and they have terrific support and knowledge bases.

Keep in mind that website-loading speed is critical for SEO, UX (user experience), and conversions. Loading speed is a part of Google's Core Web Vitals, and countless studies have proven that loading speed affects conversion rates.

For example, according to one study, 47% of consumers expect a webpage to load in 2 seconds or less (Cloudflare, 2022).

This was proven when Amazon found that for every additional 100 milliseconds in page load time, it cost them 1% in sales. That may not sound like much until you learn that a 1% loss of annual revenue for Amazon is worth BILLIONS of dollars!

Moral of the story? Speed kills.

Consider Using GenerateBlocks

You can use WordPress's native Gutenberg to build great pages (without coding), but GenerateBlocks will make your life much easier. Yes, it's a small investment, but it has one of the most powerful features: the Pattern Library.

In short, it gives you pre-built blocks you can use for your page design. They're super customizable and allow you to avoid building from scratch. I can't recommend it enough.

There are many other website builders, but 90% of them are slow, clunky, and likely to hurt loading speed.

Install Critical WordPress Plugins

The more plugins you use, the slower your website will be. It's okay initially, but always try to find custom solutions instead of using plugins. Sometimes you need a little coding, but you won't need to use unnecessary plugins. With that said, there are some mandatory plugins you'll need to get the most out of WordPress:

SEO Plugin

It's a matter of preference, but the best options are All-in-One SEO Pack, Yoast, and RankMath. I've always used the All-in-One SEO pack because I prefer its user interface (UI). However, you should test all three and see which one you prefer.

Contact Form Plugin

The three most popular contact form plugins are WPForms, Contact Form 7 and GravityForms. GravityForms is a paid option but is much more powerful. You can always start with WPForms or Contact Form 7 and upgrade to GravityForms when ready. In short, you need a contact form for your lead generation pages and your contact page.

Loading Speed Plugin

There are many caching plugins to choose from, like W3 Total Cache (free) and WP Rocket (paid). They all pretty much do the same thing. So, it's a matter of preference. We've seen great results with WP Rocket. If you choose SiteGround, you can also use their native plugins for loading speed.

Security Plugin

We use Wordfence for website security. Once again, there are many you can choose from. All that matters is to pick one because there are hackers who want into your website. These security plugins will prevent most attacks.

So those are your essential plugins. Since too many plugins will weigh down your website and make it slower, I recommend looking for custom solutions before installing more plugins than the ones mentioned above.

Install Google Analytics & Search Console

Google Analytics is essential for tracking traffic and conversions. You'll want to use Google Search Console to optimize for technical SEO. Follow Google's instructions on how to install both.

Test Creating Your Website with AI

I've tested 10web.io, which allows you to create WordPress websites with one click using AI. Definitely worth checking out if you're not comfortable building something from scratch.

Chapter 6:
Create a 1-Pager

"Never stop testing, and your advertising will never stop improving." – David Oglivy

The "1-Pager" literally means a one-page website that is a simple lead capture page that you'll use to drive all traffic to your website. You don't need a huge fancy website with hundreds of pages. You only need one strong page demonstrating why the prospect or lead should work with you and what you have to offer.

I'll walk you through an example of the keyword phrase "St Louis SEO Consultant."

Write Copy

Open up a Google Doc and get ready to write. You can also put bullet points together and outsource the writing. Also, don't worry about editing, design, or aesthetics. Instead, focus on research and writing because we'll handle that part later on.

There are some core points you'll want to touch on.

Section 1: Above the Fold

First, write your headline and sub-headline, which will go above the fold. If you're targeting a keyword, place the keyword in the headline. Then place some variations in the sub-headline.

Hey 👋 I'm the #1 St Louis SEO Consultant

———

Need more #1 rankings in Google? We rank #1 for "St Louis SEO Consultant" and we'll help you rank for your most important keywords too. Get started 🔼

Get Your Free SEO Diagnosis

Keep in mind that the following sections are the flow I like to use. Don't feel like you need to copy verbatim. Instead, use what I'm laying out as a blueprint and add or subtract based on your preferences.

Section 2: Why SEO?

Why should a business invest in SEO?

I recommend laying out the reasons in a list format like "5 Reasons Why Your St Louis Business Needs SEO."

5 Reasons Why Your St Louis Business Needs SEO (In 2022)

> **It Can Be Your #1 Growth Channel**

I've built many businesses using nothing but Search Engine
Optimization as my core digital marketing channel. We've also turned
SEO into the #1 digital marketing growth channel for 100s of St Louis,
MO companies.

And want to know what's cool when Search Engine Optimization is your
#1 digital marketing channel?

You're not reliant on expensive ads that become more difficult with each
passing day.

And you'll experience this:

Section 3: Solutions

How are you going to help them get closer to their SEO
goals? Show what your solutions are and why they can
help them. Less is more. Focus on one to three core SEO
solutions here.

Our St Louis

SEO Services.

Local SEO Service

Want to dominate your local search area (like St Louis, Missouri) and
capture all the best leads and customers? Our local SEO services rank
small St Louis businesses in Google's local search pack and the organic
results. That means you can occupy more real estate for your most
important keywords.

Section 4: Social Proof

In this section, you'll want proof that you know what you're
doing. I recommend keyword rankings, traffic growth
screenshots, mini case studies, or client testimonials.

Continue to add to this section as you build more authority.

We Practice What We Preach

Our SEO system gets big results for our clients & media websites. Take a look:

Section 5: Why You?

Why should the business work with you instead of your competitors? What's unique about your service? Be specific here.

In A Sea Of St Louis SEO Consultants, Why Us?

> **Results, Not Silly Deliverables**

Do you care if a St Louis SEO company updated your title tag? As a business, you care about results from your Internet marketing efforts. That's why we focus on high-impact actions that will deliver the best results (long-term). Not all actions are equal in Search Engine Optimization. So instead of nonsense deliverables, we focus on what works.

Speaking of results, here's a taste of what we can do:

Section 6: About You

Who are you, and why are you qualified to do SEO? Introduce yourself (or your team) and explain your qualifications.

About Gotch SEO

Hey, my name is Nathan Gotch, and I started Gotch SEO in 2013 when I was fired from my security guard job. I had no traffic, no leads, no clients, and I was $40,000 in debt. But in six months, I grew Gotch SEO to $20,000/mo, and now it's a 7-figure business. I've helped 100s of businesses in the most competitive verticals like health, legal, SAAS, and B2B get #1 rankings and more traffic. I also have one of the most popular SEO blogs in the world. And my SEO YouTube channel has over 1 million views. My SEO expertise is featured on Semrush, Ahrefs, and Search Engine Journal. But I'm most proud of the community we're building with Gotch SEO Academy. We see new SEO success stories daily, and I would love for you to join us.

Section 7: Frequently Asked Questions

What are some questions that prospects tend to ask? Tackle these questions upfront in this section.

Frequently Asked Questions

How much does SEO cost for a St Louis business?

Before I explain, it's important to reframe this question. Search Engine Optimization is NOT a cost. It is an investment. You put $1 in when it works and get $2 + out.

Now I will say this:

Working with the wrong partner will turn SEO into a cost.

In fact:

Edit with Hemingway

Once you've written your copy, I recommend running it through Hemingway Editor (hemingwayapp.com).

The tool will force you to write clean, fluff-free content.

Optimize with Grammarly

Once you've finished Hemingway edits, it's time for the final edit with Grammarly.

Again, your goal should be to get a 95 + score here.

Optimize with Rankability

Now that the edits are complete, you need to optimize the page from an SEO perspective. That's where Rankability comes in.

Go to Rankability and navigate to the Content Optimizer tool.

Copy and paste your content into the Content Optimizer.

Then go through the recommendations until you've pushed your score into the green zone.

Not Comfortable Writing? Try ChatGPT

ChatGPT is a powerful tool with tons of use cases in SEO. But it's extremely powerful if you aren't a confident writer. Just feed it solid prompts, and it'll produce something you can work with. It won't be perfect, but it's a solid foundation to build upon.

Client Communication 101

"You've got to start with the customer experience and work back toward the technology, not the other way around." — Steve Jobs

On a scale of 1 to 10 of importance, how well do you communicate with SEO leads and is an absolute 10

Why?

Because you can have all the hard skills of SEO (i.e. technical ability) but without the soft skills of knowing how to communicate effectively with your prospects and customers, you have no chance at closing and keeping clients long-term.

But thanks to technology, the good news is that it's easier than ever to streamline your client communication.

Here are some helpful tools to consider:

Calendly or ScheduleOnce

You need the ability for leads to book appointments on your calendar. It's the best way to eliminate all kinds of back-and-forth. In short, you embed your calendar, they pick a time that works, then you have a discovery call via the phone, Google Meet, or Zoom.

Google Meet or Zoom

You can't go wrong with either, except that Google Meet is free. It also integrates with all the other Google services like Gmail and Google Drive. But Zoom allows you to record meetings automatically, which allows you to review your performance.

Think about how professional athletes review tapes of their games. They're studying their performance to see how they can improve. Then in the next game, they make adjustments and act accordingly.

Selling is like a game. You can optimize and improve as you put in the reps. But you need to measure your performance on calls.

For example, what were some of the sticking points you encountered? What were some questions you didn't prepare for? Did you answer every question with conviction? How was your demeanor on the call? Were you excited or monotone? Were you friendly? Did you lay out the following steps or leave them in the air?

There are tons of questions you can ask, but start with these. Also, use your intuition and leave your ego at the door.

Everyone sucks at sales or any new skill in the beginning.

Once you get over the hump, you'll build confidence, and your sales ability will climb. We'll talk more about sales later.

Gmail

You can use any email service, but using Google's ecosystem is hard to beat. Email is best for the initial contact with a client. It's also great for your weekly or bi-weekly communication during the SEO campaign.

Video calls are best for discovery calls, proposal presentations, kickoff calls, and monthly check-ins. Everything else happens through email.

Google Voice or Grasshopper

You can manage the entire sales and fulfillment process through Zoom or Google Meet.

But some people do prefer a simple phone call.

There are two great options: Google Voice and Grasshopper.

Once again, Google Voice will integrate with all the other Google products. It's also super affordable. You can also receive and make calls from your computer with Google Voice. Grasshopper is also an excellent service, requires a separate application, and is one hundred percent mobile.

Both services allow you to select a phone number in your local area, and every call will redirect to your phone.

How NOT to Communicate with Clients

While it may seem like a trustworthy move to give out your personal cell phone number, it's not wise. All it takes is one nightmare client calling or texting you repeatedly about SEO at 11:00 p.m. for you to realize this. I speak from experience, so please don't do it.

Keep your business and personal affairs separate. You should have boundaries with clients. Will they always respect them? No.

That's why setting expectations about how you communicate is critical. You can eliminate most headaches in the kickoff call, which I'll explain later.

PART THREE:

Attack & Attract

"To keep a customer demands as much skill as to win one." –
American Proverb

Now that the foundation is down, it's time to start getting leads and clients.

I break this process into two parts: Attack and Attract.

In the Attack phase, you will be on the offensive, trying to get clients. Being on the offensive is critical initially because you won't have inbound channels built yet.

I recommend staying in the Attack phase while you're building channels for the Attract phase.

The Attract phase is when you'll attract leads and clients through inbound marketing.

Let's start with the Attack phase.

5 Keys to Success for "Attack"

1. Kill the Ego

Rejection is the only guarantee for this phase. It comes in many different forms: ghosting, outright "no," or even hostility.

That's good because it means you're taking action.

You cannot let ego dictate your behavior. Don't take it

personally. Repeat to yourself, "It's just business."

The attack phase aims to get leads and clients as fast as possible.

2. Focus on Output

Set winnable targets every day. Whether reaching out to local businesses or applying on Upwork, rig the game to make it winnable.

Don't say, *"I'm going to apply for one hundred jobs daily."*

Lofty goals are not sustainable. Instead, keep it simple.

Your goal should be, *"I'm going to submit one awesome Upwork proposal every day for the next 30 days."* Once you've proven that you can submit one daily, consider ramping it up to two.

But don't try to scale when you haven't yet accomplished the bare minimum.

3. Test → Iterate → Test

What I'm giving you in this book is a starting point. It's what worked for me. But at the end of the day, you need to build on what I'm giving you.

That means you need to test, iterate, and test even more. Testing and learning are the keys to success. Or in other words, taking action and learning from those actions makes you more effective.

So many people try to predict success through more "planning and research." But the problem is that you can't predict what will work.

You can only act and see the impact of those actions. If they're negative outcomes, adjust. If they are positive, do more of what works.

Simple, but not easy.

But once you understand that entrepreneurship is one massive project with constant twists and turns, it becomes easier to act. Keep in mind that failure is your greatest teacher in entrepreneurship.

Those who fail the most are those that take the most action. As a result, you'll learn way faster than the people who spend all their time researching and trying to predict the future.

Move fast and break stuff.

4. WIIFM

The simplest concept you can master in business is "What's In It For Me" or WIIFM.

Everything you do should start with this question: What is the other person going to get from this relationship?

Most people approach partnerships and relationships thinking about what they will get, not what the other person will receive. And that's why most people aren't successful in business.

Thinking about what another person will gain goes against human behavior.

If you study any human behavioral psychology, it's clear that humans are self-interested (Harvard, 2022). We all are. But it's not beneficial in business because adding value to other people generates income.

You add value to someone's life, and they give you money in exchange for that value.

So, if you aren't earning as much as you want, look at the value exchange. Always think about what the other person will gain before you think about what you'll gain.

5. Focus on Pain

"Twist the knife," as they say.

What it means is to focus on what pain the prospect has. In particular, the pain from not investing in SEO or not getting results. It's simple.

They're missing out on potential leads and sales if they aren't doing SEO. If they're doing SEO but failing, the outcome is the same. Their competitors beat them, and they're missing out on new business.

Remember that businesses don't care about technical SEO jargon like SSL certificates or "Core Web Vitals." They only care about SEO because it's a means to an end.

The end is more revenue without paying for expensive advertising.

So, when you're trying to market or sell to prospects, focus on what matters; more money.

Chapter 7:
Methods of "Attack"

"Are you behind on your credit card bills? Good. Pick up the phone and start dialing. Is your landlord ready to evict you? Good. Pick up the phone and start dialing. Does your girlfriend think you're a loser? Good. Pick up the phone and start dialing!" - The Wolf of Wall Street

In this section, I'll show you a few proven ways to get your first handful of clients even when no one knows who you are. These early clients are critical for building your portfolio and getting real-world experience. Be willing to do whatever it takes to get these clients. Sometimes it means working for less than you're worth. That's okay.

To put it in perspective, my first client paid me $100/month. Now my minimum retainer is $5,000/month. But that didn't happen overnight. I started at $100/month, then $250/month, then $500/month, and slowly moved up the ladder as I gained more experience.

Think about it this way: it's basic supply and demand. When you have no clients, your supply (time) is high, and demand is low. Therefore, your value is low. But when you have many clients, your supply is low, and your demand is high. Your time is more valuable, so you need to raise your prices.

Tap Into Your Close Network

Starting out, the best way to get SEO leads is from your close network. Your family, friends, and coworkers may need help or at least know someone who does. Start here, and don't be afraid to ask. You get zero of the opportunities you don't ask for. Give it a shot.

After that, you should consider posting on your social media profiles. Most people have at least a hundred people who follow them on social. Even if you only have a tiny social network, you might as well use it to your advantage.

So go ahead and post on your channels and see if you can get some leads. Don't overthink this. It can be as simple as posting that you just started a new SEO or digital marketing business that specializes in helping business owners rank their websites on the first page of Google.

Another quick reminder: think about WIIFM. Why would someone send you leads? What are they going to get out of it (besides helping a friend/family member out)?

You may want to consider a financial incentive. For example, if they send you a lead (that you close), they'll get 25% of the first month's retainer.

Upwork

Upwork is one of the best places to land new SEO clients when you're new. You have people who are looking for SEO help. All you have to do is apply and be consistent. I will show you several ways to increase your success rate on Upwork.

But here's the deal: the key to success on Upwork (or with your SEO company in general) is to do great work. In other words, actually deliver results for your clients.

That leads to strong reviews and positive word of mouth. But everything begins and ends with results.

Start with Your Upwork Profile

The first place to start is with your profile. Believe it or not, your profile isn't as important as you think.

The biggest factor that clients look for is your reviews. Of course, you can use fancy copywriting tactics, but you won't get far without social proof.

That's why you need to make it a priority to get as many reviews as possible. And that means you'll need to work for less than what you believe you're worth. But the point is to land clients, deliver results, and get reviews as fast as possible. Then, you'll have the social proof you need to win even more clients.

The question is, how do you land that initial pool of clients when you have no reviews? Well, you'll need to narrow the gaps in other ways.

Get A Professional Headshot

First, you need to get a professional headshot. There are only two options: hire a professional or do it yourself.

According to City Headshots, it ranges between $150 to $2,500 for professional headshots (City Headshots, 2022).

The benefit of hiring a professional is that they'll do a good job. Plus, you won't need to learn an unnecessary skill (that will take away from other things you need to focus on).

But if your budget is tight, you can do it yourself. All you need is an iPhone or DSLR camera.

For example, the headshot below is from a DSLR camera, taken by my wife:

I use the same DSLR camera to record YouTube videos.

I'm not a photographer, but here are some critical factors to get a solid headshot.

Your Appearance is Critical

Think about who you're trying to influence to become a client. Most prospects are professionals and businesspeople. They expect you to look professional. You've heard the idea that you shouldn't judge a book by its cover. While that's cute and all, it's what people do. Studies have shown that someone's appearance can influence people's behavior.

In one study, they found that *"physicians wearing white coats were perceived as significantly more experienced, professional, and friendly compared with those wearing fleece or softshell jackets" (JAMA Netw Open, 2021).*

The point is that people will judge you and draw conclusions about you before you say a single word. So, the adage is true: dress to impress. Don't try to be Mark Zuckerberg.

Once you're looking professional, it's time to take some pictures. Find a blank white or off-white wall for the background to remove it in the edits. Canva removes backgrounds, but don't worry about that for now.

The next critical piece is lighting. Again, there are two options: natural light and artificial. You can buy a cheap light on Amazon, which will do the job (if natural lighting isn't an option). Search "photography lighting" to get some options.

Lastly, you'll need someone to take your pictures. I won't get into how to take headshots, but Google is your best friend.

Once your headshot is ready, you need to tap into Upwork search.

Optimize for Search

SEO doesn't only apply to Google. It applies to any website with a search function. For example, Upwork is a search-driven website.

And you need to show up when business owners are searching for SEO.

The good news is that optimizing your Upwork profile for search is easy.

Keep in mind that reviews are a big piece of the puzzle. The reason is simple: Upwork wants to suggest a freelancer with a proven track record. If Upwork does this well, people will keep using the platform. So Upwork is incentivized to deliver the best freelancers for any given task.

Your reviews are low initially, so you'll need to make up gaps on other fronts. Here's how to optimize your Upwork profile.

First, place your keyword in the title and first sentence.

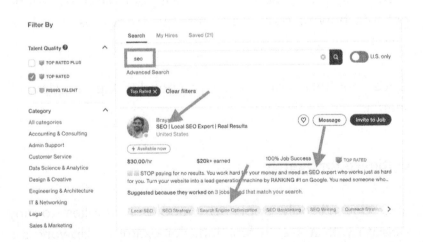

Second, write a deep description explaining what you do. Note: The profile below is just an example, you should research many profiles on Upwork to model yours after.

SEO | Local SEO Expert | Real Results $30.00/hr

STOP paying for no results. You work hard for your money and need an SEO expert who works just as hard for you. Turn your website into a lead generation machine by RANKING #1 on Google.

You need someone who understands Search Engine Optimization and can solve all of your SEO problems. I take a communication-based approach to my work. I'll walk you through each step of the plan so that you're not in the dark during the process.

... WHAT YOU WILL GET: ...
No more time wasted
No more money wasted
Consistent updates (No more wondering what your SEO specialist is working on)
Real results
Competitor analysis
Optimized URLs
Optimized Alt text
Imaged Alt text
H1-H6 title tags
Optimized content

REVIEWS FROM CLIENTS
"Brayam was absolutely wonderful from start to finish! He did just what I asked for, he made suggestions and implemented those as well!!! Very pleased!!! If you're looking for someone to handle your SEO, to get you on the right path, he is the man for the job! We will hire him again!"

"Brayam is so different from every other "SEO specialist" who promises you the world but never goes anywhere. I would recommend him and I have gotten great results".

VALUES:
Providing the best customer service
100% White Hat and Natural SEO
Always providing top-notch content
A proven solution to generate results
Data-driven

TOOLS I USE:
Ahrefs
Semrush
Google Analytics
Google Search Console
Page Optimizer Pro
Screaming Frog SEO

SKILLS INCLUDE
On-page SEO
Off-page
Technical SEO
White hat backlink
Sitemaps
Structured Data
Schema Markup

About Me:
I am a result-driven SEO expert specializing in lead generation. Organic Google search is the best and most cost-effective way to generate leads because you don't constantly have to keep spending money on ads.

I have worked with local businesses, software companies, service-based businesses to increase their traffic and grow their call count and leads from their website and Google My Business.

If you think we'd be a good fit to work together, invite me to submit a proposal or reach out to me and we can talk more about your business's needs. Every business is different; we can work together to create a plan that caters to your needs. I would like to get to know you and your business to be able to better assist you!
less

(Upwork, 2022)

Then use the following actions to increase the depth of your profile even further:

Create A Professional Intro Video

The way to add depth to your Upwork profile is to create a professional intro video.

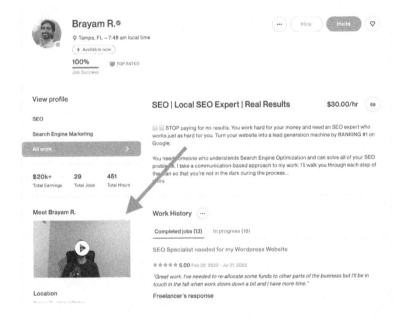

I know video is a frightening concept. But it's not the future; it's now. You need to get comfortable with video because it is a powerful tool to grow your business.

YouTube is the second biggest driver of leads in my SEO business. And I used to be deathly afraid of video. So if you want to stand out, get out of your comfort zone and create a simple profile video (make sure you have good lighting and a solid mic).

Story time:

Back in 2015, I signed up for the Yelp partner program – don't do it. As part of the program, they sent a videographer to film me talking about my business. Unfortunately, I was a deer in the headlights and couldn't formulate intelligent thoughts.

It was such an embarrassing experience, I declared I would never do video again because I sucked so bad at it.

Fortunately, I got over it and eventually overcame my fear and decided to start recording. But I took baby steps. First, I recorded hundreds of videos using slide presentations but never showed my face. That gave me decent confidence. Then I started recording some talking head videos. And guess what?

I still sucked.

But for every video I recorded, I gained a little more confidence and the videos slowly improved. And now I have zero fear of recording videos. But it's all because I made a conscious decision to get back on camera.

Unfortunately, there's no hack or trick for this.

You must press record to overcome your fear and get better on video. The faster you dive in, the quicker you'll be successful. Do yourself a favor and go take a look at your favorite YouTubers first videos from years ago. It's like night and day.

Getting back to your Upwork intro video, keep it simple.

Explain who you are, what types of projects you work on, and your areas of expertise.

Make sure it's no more than five minutes. The goal of the video is to show that you're a real person, and you'll build a connection with the prospect much faster.

Also, appearing on video is funny because of the "celebrity effect." People tend to have a higher perception of you because you're on video. It's a weird but very real thing.

Let me put it this way: If you get anything from this book, please start recording more videos. I can't recommend it enough.

Get Testimonials

Testimonials will be hard to come by in the beginning. But social proof is one of the most powerful forms of persuasion so it needs to be a priority. The question is, how do you get more?

You need to work for less than you're worth. It's that simple. Your number-one goal, in the beginning, is to earn as many testimonials and reviews as possible.

You also need to get results so you can build case studies, which makes the lead generation and sales process much easier.

The more results and testimonials you get, the easier it becomes to get clients.

Use Simple, Persuasive Copywriting

You don't need to be an expert-level copywriter to create persuasive copy. You need to understand some of the core tenets of persuasion.

I recommend reading two books: *Influence and Cashvertising*.

Both will teach you how to be more persuasive.

With that said, I'll focus on some of the elements you can leverage today.

Social Proof

Notice how many times I talked about testimonials, reviews, and case studies? It's because it taps into the superpower of social proof. People trust other people's experiences with products or services. Transparency sells. That's why I rank it as the most crucial persuasion vehicle.

Authority

Would you trust health advice from your family doctor wearing a lab coat over some guy wearing a white t-shirt and jeans? In most cases, the answer is yes. This is the power of perceived authority. But you don't need a Ph.D. to establish yourself as an authority in your vertical. You can do it using a few different techniques.

The fastest way is to write some guest posts on well-known websites or participate in HARO (Help a Reporter Out) to get exposure on influential or authoritative sites. We'll dig deeper into this in the lead generation chapter.

Liking

Do you have good vibes, and are you likable? If not, you might as well pack up and quit now. Kidding. It's hard to quantify, but you should focus on increasing your energy levels and friendliness. People (and clients) are attracted to positive, friendly individuals. It's not about pretending to be someone else – just kill them with kindness and you really can't go overboard here.

You'll notice this when you record a video.

You may think and feel that you're being over-the-top with your high-energy persona. But when you watch the recording, you'll see that your energy isn't as intense as you thought. In most cases, you'll just appear more upbeat and positive (and likable).

Keep in mind that people also like people who are like them. So always look for similarities between you and your prospects.

Reciprocity

Have you ever noticed that companies offer free consultations or free demos? They're not trying to be your friend. Instead, they're tapping into reciprocity. Giving something away for free gives you a reason to become a lead.

Most people feel a need to repay the debt when given something. It's subconscious. For example, if you watch a valuable YouTube video, you may feel obliged to give something in return to the creator. You may like the video, leave a comment, or even subscribe to their newsletter.

When you give free value, you tend to get positive influence back. That's why creating free content is so effective.

Create a Unique Offer

You don't need to reinvent the wheel to stand out from the crowd. But in any business, a little creativity can attract a lot of attention which can lead to more clients and sales.

You must do the same when trying to win on Upwork. When you're starting out, offer a free SEO audit or site analysis. Or offer a free 30-minute SEO consultation. Be creative here, but the key word here is free.

Get Certified

Earning certifications is another powerful way to get more credibility. Think about how doctors hang their educational certificates in their offices. It's a signal of authority and trust. So, try to earn every relevant and credible certificate you can and post it on your Upwork profile.

For example, we have three SEO certificates inside our training program Gotch SEO Academy: SEO Specialist, SEO Expert, and SEO Mastery Certifications.

Our members can earn diplomas and then plaster them on

Upwork and social media such as LinkedIn. As a result, it builds tremendous credibility and trust by showing they've put in the work to become better at their craft.

The point is to earn as many legitimate certifications as possible. You can never have too many. And this is important in the beginning when you likely won't have a lot of testimonials or social proof.

Find Jobs

Now that your profile is ready, it's time to look for SEO job opportunities.

Go to the Upwork search bar, select "Apply for Jobs Posted by Clients," and start searching for opportunities.

Use keywords like "SEO," "Search Engine Optimization," "Link Building," etc.

You can then use advanced filters to find the best opportunities.

First, consider using the "Payment Verified" filter, which proves the client is legit, and you'll actually get paid. Unfortunately, like anything else, there are some bad actors on the platform.

Second, consider filtering by "Number of Proposals." Prioritize listings with less competition first. Then work your way through the other ones.

I recommend sending a minimum of one quality proposal per day. That's 365 proposals in a year. Even if you only convert at 1%, you'll still have four new clients to work with.

Create Proposals

Apply and Reply Fast

Speed is the name of the game on Upwork. Yes, the quality of your proposal matters. But the clock is ticking once a new opportunity pops up. That's why you need to check daily and apply within twenty-four hours. I would check every hour during the work day in the beginning. And if you get a response, reply ASAP.

Personalize. Personalize. Personalize.

While speed is essential, personalization is even more critical. Therefore, do not send templated, generic applications.

Yes, it's a number game, but you must take each proposal seriously. Read the entire job listing and respond to specific parts. Be careful of tricky things that job posters will do (like me).

I often say, "Write the word 'carrot' in your proposal." And then anyone who doesn't write "carrot" gets ignored. So why would I play this game? Because it shows attention to detail and how much they care about this opportunity.

Think about it: How will they perform at their job if someone can't even read a proposal with a moderate level of attention? So make sure YOU pay attention and try to go the extra mile when submitting your proposals.

CTA

Every proposal should have a clear call to action (CTA). The key is reciprocity here. You need an exchange of value that motivates the hiring manager to consider your proposal. I recommend a free SEO audit and a free SEO consultation to discuss your findings. It's the best way to demonstrate your expertise, give free value, and build goodwill.

You don't need to "sell." You need to add more value than your competition.

Keep It Simple (for the Employer)

Don't write a dissertation. Instead, keep your proposal lean but effective and hit all the critical persuasion points. The hiring managers likely won't read much of your proposal. Instead, they'll go to your profile and decide based on that.

But here's something important. If you're new, acknowledge it in your proposal.

I'm new on Upwork, but I'll prove to you that I'm the right fit for your SEO campaign.

Here's my simple offer:

I'll perform a free SEO audit and give you actionable recommendations for getting better rankings and more traffic. Then we'll have a free SEO consultation to discuss my findings. So give me a shot, and you won't regret it! The audit and consultation are free, so you have nothing to lose :).

The point is to make your shortcomings your advantage. Don't pretend to be bigger than you are. Use the fact that you're new and not a massive company as a positive since you can give a more personal touch than a huge agency can.

Also, I would aim for one to three hundred words for your proposal. Less is more when you hit the right points.

Use Video If Possible

Once again, you should have your intro video on your profile. But a short two to three-minute, personalized video can be enough to win deals on Upwork. I've hired people who took the time to record a video with their proposals. It shows that you care about the project and are willing to do whatever it takes.

The key is to personalize it. Say the company's name, mention some details in their job listing, and pitch a solid offer, like a free SEO audit.

Dig Through Job Boards

Upwork is the most popular platform for earning freelance SEO jobs, but you should also keep tabs on digital job boards. They're similar to Upwork, and the process is the same.

Create Profiles

Here's a list of job boards to create profiles for:

- Clarity.fm
- Freelancer.com
- Peopleperhour.com
- Remotive.com
- Marketerhire.com
- Fiverr.com
- Thumbtack.com
- Guru.com
- Freeup.net

Aim to create one profile per day until you've covered all of them. Then, you can use the same content from your Upwork profile.

Establish A Small, Winnable Target

Like Upwork, you need to set winnable targets. Shoot for one proposal per day on at least one job board. So, at this point, you'll be doing two proposals per day at a minimum, one for Upwork and one for a job board. It shouldn't take any more than an hour per day to hit your targets. Keep in mind that these are the bare minimum. You'll want to scale this up if you're serious about getting clients in a short amount of time.

Conclusion

When you don't have a portfolio, you need to be scrappy. Fight tooth and nail to build your portfolio as fast as possible. There is no shortage of opportunities in the SEO industry. All you must do is take small actions every day. This "Attack" phase isn't forever (unless you want it to be).

The goal of this phase is to simply build your portfolio while the "Attract" methods are built. Then, eventually, 99% of your leads will come to you instead of you seeking them out. But like my business partner Simon always says, "You gotta eat some dirt before you get to the carrot."

Chapter 8:
Attract

"My definition of marketing is: getting someone who has a need, to know, like, and trust you." – John Jantsch

---

The "Attack" phase will help you get your first handful of clients. These clients are critical because you'll leverage your results to get even more clients. The key word here is **results**.

Results are the only thing that clients care about, and it's your biggest point of leverage.

But if you can show clients relevant results, now you're cooking with fire.

For example, if you're targeting plumbers, show SEO results from plumbing companies. It's a simple concept, but it makes a huge difference. With that said, you'll need to continue the "Attack" phase while building up the "Attract" phase.

The "Attract" phase is simple: **traffic, leads, and clients will come to you instead of you chasing them down**. Some people refer to this as inbound marketing. It is the holy grail of growing a business.

Now the reason why I'm introducing this phase second is that each method takes time. Think of each Attract method as planting seeds. You need to start planting seeds today to enjoy the fruits of your labor in the future.

But before I show you the methods, you'll need to understand a few key concepts about digital marketing.

Funnels

"The sales team owns the sales funnel. But as a B2B marketer, you feed the top of their funnel." – Doug Kessler

A traditional sales funnel has four parts, starting at the top with **Awareness**. At this stage, your goal is to drive awareness for your brand. It is not to sell. The best way to drive brand awareness is through content.

In short, you'll create free, unique value on your blog, YouTube, or even Twitter. As a result, people will start to look at you as a trusted advisor and authority on the subject matter. Do this over an extended period, and you'll build an audience.

That leads to the next stage of the funnel, which is **Interest**. At this point, a prospect is interested in what you have to offer. But your content needs to be different.

In the context of getting SEO clients, case studies work best at this stage. An example would be: "Discover How this Chiropractor Grew His Practice by 134% (Without Advertising)." I recommend gating this content (i.e. hiding it behind a lead capture form) so they have to submit their name and email address to get access.

Once they've consumed your top of the funnel (aka ToFu – brand awareness content) and middle of the funnel (aka MoFu – interest-based content) you'll need to focus one hundred percent on building desire through social proof, which leads to the **Decision** phase of the funnel. At this point, it's your job to convert them into a Sales Qualified Lead (SQL). Testimonials (the more relevant, the better), demos, and FAQs work best at this stage.

You'll need to work on optimizing lead generation pages if they're not converting but let's say you get someone to submit a lead form; now it's time for the final stage or bottom of the funnel (aka BoFu), which is **Action**.

During the Action stage, your goal is to turn the SQL into a client. I'll show you my complete closing process later on.

Note: Don't let the terminology on this page intimidate you. What's important is to understand that your client relationship is a journey starting with Awareness (learning about you) and ultimately leading to Action (becoming your client).

Use SEO

"A website without SEO is like a vehicle without fuel." -
Ravinder Bharti

I know it's a crazy idea, but imagine using the exact same channel you're trying to sell. Well, that's what I did in the beginning.

I ranked for keywords like "Santa Monica SEO," "Glendale SEO," and "St Louis SEO" in 2014, and they still rank to this day. These keywords produce qualified leads for SEO services.

So, look at your local area. If your site is new, focus on the smaller cities first. Then go after the bigger cities.

If you're targeting a niche, you need to dominate Google for all your most important niche keywords, like "SEO for chiropractors."

There are two main techniques you can use to get more clients using SEO:

1. Build A Hyper-Focused Website

Instead of building a huge website, you can get clients with a hyper-focused one. For example, I own the domain stlouisseoconsultant.com, an Exact Match Domain (EMD). These keyword-rich domains work exceptionally well on the local SEO level.

The idea is to score easy rankings without being super skilled or needing a ton of website authority. For example, stlouisseoconsultant.com only has one page on the entire website.

You can duplicate this strategy on the local level or even on the niche level.

For example, let's say you were targeting chiropractors. You can get a domain like "chiropractorseopro.com," and then once properly optimized, you'd show up whenever your ideal clients (chiropractors) search for SEO services. I'll dive into deeper SEO strategies later in this book.

But building a hyper-focused website is best when you're one hundred percent focused on ranking in Google. However, the next option is best if you're thinking longer-term and want to build a solid brand.

2. Build An Authority Website

You can still target locations and niches on your authority website (a website that focuses on one, broad topic like SEO, fitness, or technology). It's just a different approach.

For example, GotchSEO.com ranks for "St Louis SEO" and "SEO for chiropractors," which proves that authority websites give you more flexibility in your SEO strategy. At any time, I can target new niches for landing SEO clients.

The same is not true for the hyper-focused strategy. With a hyper-focused website, you must stay one hundred percent on the topic to be most effective. But building an authority website does have some downsides.

First, it's a long-term play. Which means you'll need to focus on building website authority through link-building to make your website effective from an SEO perspective.

Second, you'll sacrifice relevance. Hyper-focused websites perform well because they're highly relevant to specific searches. Google is a relevance machine. It wants to show searchers the most relevant, high-quality results possible. However, having an EMD won't be enough to rank in Google. You still need backlinks to rank, but it will be less than a branded domain that doesn't contain exact match keywords.

The good news?

This isn't a life-or-death decision. You can use both techniques (which I recommend).

3. Bonus: Use Both Techniques

I recommend building a hyper-focused website because you'll get results faster. However, you should also consider building your primary brand website at the same time. That way, you're acting on both short and long-term goals.

Many successful agencies deploy this strategy. First, they have their main brand website and then build hyper-focused websites. For example, Timmermann Group, an agency in St Louis executes this extremely well. They have one primary agency site, WeAreTG.com. Then they have hyper-focused websites like STLWebDesignCo.com.

Keep in mind that you build these hyper-focused websites for one reason: ranking and lead generation. Many successful SEOs have done it (including yours truly) and you can do the same.

YouTube

"You don't even need to go college no more because you could learn how to do everything on YouTube." – Janet Evanovich

Here's the thing:

Almost no one uses YouTube to drive leads for their SEO businesses. And this is a huge mistake. YouTube is one of our top sources of lead generation in our business.

The challenge is that people think they need to become full-time YouTubers to get results. Not true. What you need to do is become strategic and use YouTube to attract your ideal customers.

So instead of creating broad content like "What is SEO?" create hyper-focused content for your ideal customer.

Let's say you're targeting HVAC companies. You want to become the go-to authority on "HVAC SEO." If I were building a channel and wanted to attract perfect leads, I would create videos like:

"11 Actionable SEO Tips for HVAC Companies (in {YEAR})"

This content angle is one hundred percent informational. You're overwhelming them with free value to build goodwill, trust, and authority. If you do this well, you don't need calls to action in your video. Here's what a sample intro could look like:

> *Hey, this is Nathan from HVAC SEO Pros, and in this video, I'll show you eleven actionable SEO techniques that are working right now to grow your HVAC business. And make sure you watch until the end because 99% of HVAC companies ignore tip number eight (and it's killing their rankings).*

I'm telling you from experience that you don't need to jam CTAs down people's throats. Plus, YouTube will kill your video performance if it's too commercial. Instead, focus on education and providing value. Then, if someone wants to work with you, they'll find a way.

Creating informational content is critical. But you must also create content that proves you know what you're doing. Of course, anyone can throw together some tips they gathered on the Internet. But it's hard to fake results.

And that's when the second content angle comes into play.

"New SEO Case Study: How to Grow Your HVAC Business by 94%"

This content angle demonstrates that you have both the expertise and solution to a problem your prospects care about. In addition, it builds trust and authority when you provide results. In short, a helpful video like this will show how you achieved the outcome step-by-step.

"7 HVAC SEO Trends for {YEAR} (This Changes Everything)"

You must position yourself as an advisor and someone on the industry's cutting edge. Presenting trends is a powerful way to accomplish this goal. People will come to you to find out "what's working right now."

"Live SEO Audit of Chicago HVAC Company ({YEAR})"

Live audits are one of the most potent content angles because viewers can watch you audit a real business. For example, you can audit a random HVAC company's website and explain what you would do to improve its SEO performance.

These are just a handful of content angles you can use on YouTube and there are many more.

But the critical point here is to FOCUS.

Yes, there's nothing wrong with building a huge following on YouTube. However, if you're doing it for lead generation and to build your SEO business, it's better to be hyper-focused and attract your ideal customers.

And there's almost no competition on YouTube for hyper-focused SEO YouTube channels. Take advantage.

Social Media

> *"The biggest thing I can tell you is that you have to make as much content as possible." – Gary Vaynerchuk*

Don't fall for the trap of being an SEO purist.

Instead, think of yourself as a digital marketer who specializes in SEO. But don't neglect other marketing channels because they can be a huge lead generation source. Here are three channels to start building a presence immediately:

LinkedIn

I've found there are a few content frameworks that work well on LinkedIn. But if you want more SEO clients, you need to be strategic with your content strategy.

First, focus on creating one piece of content daily, Monday through Friday. Use a tool like OneUp to batch-create and schedule your content. It isn't easy to come up with ideas every single day. For example, I batch create all my content for the entire month in one to two days. Then I schedule it strategically with OneUp.

Second, understand why you're posting on LinkedIn in the first place – to build your authority as an SEO expert. And you can accomplish that goal by giving free value.

As a result, people will reach out to you via LinkedIn Direct Messages (DM) or head to Google and search for you.

Here are some examples of how to do this:

1. Free Actionable Value

Short, bite-sized SEO advice works best here. I recommend writing your social media content in Hemingway and then editing it with Grammarly.

Use short sentences, and don't be generic. Generic SEO tips won't do well. Try to make it unique.

You should integrate video as well. For example, a video I posted on LinkedIn was created entirely through Canva. I recorded the voiceover with Voice Memos on my iPhone, edited it in iMovie, and used Canva for the graphics.

Anyone can do this. You can learn basic video editing skills in a day. And I highly recommend doing it because you'll be able to pump out content faster without needing a huge budget.

Then once your revenue grows, you can bring on an editor to take the load off.

2. Polarization

It's no surprise that polarizing content does well on social media. The truth is that anyone can get eyeballs by being controversial. But we're not trying to get lots of eyeballs. We're trying to get the right eyeballs so we can land clients.

So you need to create polarizing content in the context of the SEO or digital marketing industry.

You don't need to share your political or religious views. Instead, you can share "controversial" views about SEO that will spark discussion.

And when discussion occurs, views soon follow.

Warning: Use polarization sparingly. Otherwise, you'll be like Kanye West, known for always being controversial. That's not the goal. The idea to spark some healthy debate every now and then.

3. Results

The last and most important framework is to share results and case studies.

Results demonstrate authority and expertise.

These types of posts are your big conversion vehicles. So

use it as often as possible (at least once per week).

Note that my content isn't some complex SEO case study. Before and after images (showing increased rankings, etc) can work well here. Keep it simple and let the results do the talking.

Twitter

It might take you by surprise, but Twitter can be another excellent social media channel for landing new clients. Again, the process is similar to LinkedIn.

1. Polarization

Just like LinkedIn, polarizing content works well on Twitter.

I'll mention this again. You don't need to discuss broad, controversial topics to get exposure. Instead, use polarization in the context of your target industry.

For example: "If you think SEO is harder than it used to be, you're doing it wrong."

Keep in mind that my social media content broadly targets the SEO industry. However, if you're niching down, you might want to keep it even narrower.

2. Results

Once again, let your results do the talking here.

There are many armchair warriors on Twitter, so be prepared for people to question your strategies and results.

But don't fear feedback or trolls. They don't realize it, but they fuel your content's performance.

The more engagement you get, the more exposure you'll receive.

"Any press is good press" regarding maximum exposure to your content.

3. Threads

Threads are long-form content for Twitter.

In short, you string a series of Tweets together to create longer content.

It works well when used sparingly.

Sparingly is the key word here. People overuse this strategy, and it will burn your audience out.

One important tip is to add unique visual elements to your threads. For example, I like to create unique graphics with Canva for each step of a longer piece of content.

My posting cadence on Twitter varies but it can be as much as one to two times per business day or as little as once or twice per week.

But that doesn't mean you have to do the same. I recommend testing your market and going to the upper limit of what you can realistically commit to.

Remember, your goal is to stay top-of-mind with your prospects.

Start Creating & Publishing Today

Look, there are no rules on social media. Use the frameworks I've given you, but put a twist on them.

First, you need to find your own voice and style. That only happens when you hit that **Publish** button hundreds of times. There is no shortcut.

Publish, watch the performance, adjust, be patient, and most importantly, don't stop.

And lastly, don't forget why you're creating content for

social media in the first place. It's not to boost your ego by getting vanity metrics like views or likes. It's to get more clients and grow your businesses. Period. Views and likes don't pay the bills. If your content isn't driving leads, then you need to adjust.

But also, remember that social media isn't like direct-response marketing. It's much more of a brand-building play. If you do it right, many people will find you on Google through branded searches. And guess what? I can tell you from personal experience when they do, it's so much easier to close them.

That said, the sales journey or trust-building process could take weeks, months or even years. I've had people who literally consumed my content for years and then finally made the leap to become a lead.

You never know who's watching. That's why you must keep creating and publishing.

Communities

When I first started posting in online communities, I would respond to questions on sites Quora, Reddit, and Blackhatworld (not recommended). Getting clients through communities like this still works if you do it well. The key is to focus on adding value.

You must be visible almost daily by contributing helpful advice and giving useful tips to other community members. Then, and only then, people will start to notice and want to learn more about what you offer.

The worst thing you can do is jump into a group and start pitching yourself or your services right away. It almost never works. And like the methods in the "Attack" section, you should set a daily target for making offers or in this case, adding value.

For example: "I will respond to one Quora question daily." Remember: small, achievable goals.

So, what are the best communities where you could land clients?

Well, before I show you, remember what the goal is. You're trying to land clients. And your clients are often business owners, entrepreneurs, or marketing directors.

Therefore, you need to join communities where those individuals spend time.

You can easily join SEO or digital marketing communities, but only a tiny percentage of your ideal clients will be there.

Here are a few good places to post:

Reddit

There's a subreddit for pretty much every industry you can imagine. You'll need to make your presence felt in these subreddits without pitching your services. Focus on adding value without expectation. Then make sure you optimize your profile so someone can get in touch with you. You should also use the search function on Reddit to find opportunities.

Search for your target industry, like "plumber SEO" or "plumber marketing."

You should also join the "plumber" subreddits and find opportunities to add value.

Quora

Quora is the most popular question-and-answer (Q&A)

site. There are hundreds of SEO questions waiting for your answers. You can also get more granular and use Quora's search function to find threads specific to your industry.

For example, if you're targeting plumbers, search for "plumber marketing" and or "plumber SEO."

Then, create a thoughtful response. Make sure your profile is optimized and complete as well.

Business Forums

Traditional forums aren't as popular as they once were.

But, here are some to consider:

- Indiehackers.com
- producthunt.com
- thefastlaneforum.com
- startupnation.com.

There are many business owners and entrepreneurs who hang out in these forums.

If you establish yourself as a valuable SEO contributor, you can score great leads.

Email Marketing

"Email has an ability many channels don't: creating valuable, personal touches—at scale." – David Newman

---

So, here's a fact about website traffic:

Not everyone is ready to become your client. Only 1-3% of your website visitors will actually become a lead on the first visit. And that's if you're doing an exceptional job.

The reality is, most websites will convert less than 1%. That means 99% of your website visitors are leaving without taking any further action. What's even scarier is that most visitors will never return.

But don't worry, all hope is not lost. Especially when you start to understand the sales cycle.

Truth be told, most people will need nurturing to warm up to the idea of them becoming a lead for your business. Folks have told me they followed my work for years before becoming a client. They watched countless videos, read all my blog content, and even followed me on social media. Now that's an extreme example; most people don't need that much time to make a decision

But the point is that you must have an intelligent nurturing process. And it all starts with email marketing.

Email is king when it comes to driving leads and conversions. It's by far my most powerful marketing tool. And that's why I build every strategy around getting email subscribers.

It works because although most people are not ready to become your client just yet, many will give you their email in exchange for free value.

And that's why you need to develop lead magnets.

Create A Lead Magnet

A lead magnet is a gated piece of content offered in exchange for contact information, mostly email addresses. It can come in the form of a webinar, VSL (Video Sales Letter), e-book, templates, or a checklist.

Effective lead magnets can work to move the relationship deeper into the sales funnel. But since video builds a connection with viewers at a rapid rate, webinars or video content tend to nurture leads faster than a checklist, for example.

With that said, I recommend testing all formats.

But here's the key to a successful lead magnet: **<u>relevance</u>**.

Let's say you're building a focused YouTube channel about HVAC SEO. Well, you need a way to get those viewers to your site so you can convert them. Your best option is a focused lead magnet that's built for your ideal client.

Here are some examples of what I would build for an HVAC SEO business:

- **Free Ebook:** 11 Deadly SEO Sins that 99% of HVAC Businesses Are Committing Right Now

- **Free Training:** HVAC SEO Masterclass for {YEAR} - Follow this simple process and get high-quality leads and clients from Google (without paying a dime for ads)

- **Free Checklist:** The Complete HVAC SEO Checklist for {YEAR} - Follow this checklist and rank #1 in Google for your most important keyword (so you can get more high-quality leads and clients 24/7 WITHOUT paying for expensive ads).

- **Free SEO Case Study:** How We Skyrocketed Lead Volume for an HVAC Business by 137% in Only 30 Days

Get the idea? The purpose is to move the relationship from a content consumer to a legitimate prospect. You're moving them deeper into the funnel, one step at a time.

Now, what do you do after you've scored an email subscriber?

Create A Nurture Sequence

You must nurture the lead to build trust and authority. And you accomplish this through a simple, automated email sequence. Almost every email marketing software allows you to set up sequences like ConvertKit, Mailchimp, and Drip.

It doesn't matter what tool you use here. What matters is the content you deliver to your ideal prospect.

So, let's rewind and see the path the sample prospect has traveled.

1. They watched a YouTube video about HVAC SEO

2. They opted in for a free checklist about HVAC SEO

3. They've received their free download and are now an email subscriber

So far, so good.

The next step is to send them an email and I highly recommend a simple "welcome" message – state who you are, what you do, and what they can expect next.

Here's an example:

Subject Line: Thank you!

Hey Bill,

Thank you so much for signing up for my HVAC SEO news-letter! My name is John Doe, and I help HVAC businesses get more free traffic, leads, and clients from Google. Here's what one of my clients said:

"We were skeptical about investing in SEO services again because we have been burned in the past. But we took a leap of faith and decided to work with John Doe. It was the best decision for our business because our lead volume grew so much that we had to hire new team members to fulfill the requests. And that's a good problem to have! If you're an HVAC company or contractor, then there's no one else you should work with except for John." - Josh, Founder at Awesome HVAC Guys

What you can expect from me:

I'm going to send you a short HVAC SEO training series. You'll get a new email every week with the newest lesson.

Each lesson is jam-packed with actionable SEO tips. This means you can take these tips and start seeing results fast.

And if you don't want to do all this geeky SEO stuff yourself, I'm also here to help. Our company focuses 100% on SEO for HVAC companies. Click here to learn more.

Look for the following email: "The truth about HVAC SEO."

And open it as soon as you get it.

Thanks again, and talk soon!

- John Doe

[Book Your Free SEO Diagnosis]

Send this welcome email within an hour of an email subscriber signing up.

Then all you need to do is create a five to seven email sequence that drips out at a cadence of one per week.

Now you might be wondering what types of emails you should create. I've got you covered. You need to rely on the persuasion levers you learned earlier in this book.

Here are some examples:

- The truth about HVAC SEO

- How this HVAC company failed at SEO

- 435% more HVAC leads (easy SEO process)

- The right time to invest in SEO

- HVAC leads are searching right now

Notice that I don't focus too much on the process of learning SEO.

Instead, the series aims to demonstrate your authority, deliver social proof, and help them decide on hiring an SEO company.

Every email you send should include a call to action. Again, I recommend using the P.S. technique.

For example, you'll deliver value in the email. Then at the end, you'll do something like this:

- John Doe

P.S. We have a few slots this week for a free HVAC SEO diagnosis. Click here to book your spot."

Switch up these CTAs with every email.

And in the final email – *"HVAC leads are searching right now,"* you should go for a direct pitch of your services.

Add some urgency and scarcity to the offer to push them to become a lead. Some levers you can pull are limited availability or a limited-time free offer for booking a call.

To sum up, if you create a lead magnet and combine it with a simple nurture sequence, you'll be miles ahead of the 90% of SEO agencies who don't. Just remember that it's not a set-it-and-forget-it process. You'll need to review its performance and make adjustments as you go.

Get Referrals

> *"Nothing influences people more than a recommendation from a trusted friend." - Mark Zuckerberg*

All the "Attract" techniques I've shown you will get you organic traffic on autopilot. But as you've learned, most inbound traffic is cold and not ready to become a lead. This is why you need a nurturing email process in place.

But referrals and word of mouth are different.

These leads are hot because someone else recommended you. So, they're already deeper into the sales cycle and more likely to become clients. That's why it's fundamental that you make referral generation a part of your marketing strategy. Fortunately, the process for generating referrals is simple.

1. ASK!

It sounds crazy but most agencies never ask for referrals from successful, happy clients. But most clients aren't going to magically send you referrals. You have to make it happen and be willing to pop the question such as:

Subject Line: Quick question

Hey Bill,

I'm so glad to hear that you've had a great experience with us so far and look forward to helping you crush your competition!

In the meantime, could you do me a huge favor and let me know if you have any colleagues or friends who could benefit from our services?

It would really help me out and I'd love to help them achieve similar growth (plus I'll make it worth your while if they become a client ;)

If not, no worries and thank you for your business.

Talk soon,

[Your Name]

2. Create A Rewards Program

Asking is one thing; getting them to actually do it is another.

That's when incentives come in. Every client wants to be more profitable. So the best incentive is to give them a discount on their monthly retainer for every referral they send.

For example, let's say the client is paying $5,000/month. You can make a deal to give them 25% off next month's retainer for every closed deal they send your way. You might think I'm crazy for 25%, but the math is simple.

You're giving the client a $1,250 discount. But if you close another client worth $5,000/month, it's a no-brainer. Always think in terms of LTV (Lifetime Value) when measuring your CAC (Cost to Acquire Customers). Investing $1,250 to get one client might seem like a lot. However, in the context of LTV, it makes perfect sense. Let's say you retain the $5,000/month client for six months. That's $28,750 after subtracting the CAC. If you view the $1,250 as an investment, that's a 2,200% return on your money.

And keep in mind that you're only paying out a commission for closed deals. So, you literally have no risk if you implement a rewards program such as this..

3. Set A Cadence

Review your campaigns every week or month and identify clients who are eligible for your rewards program. Remember, the vast majority of clients will not send you referrals without being asked. They're as busy as you are. You need to be proactive.

Build Your Personal Brand

"Branding is what people say about you when you are not in the room." – Jeff Bezos

Every marketing method I've shown you, including SEO, YouTube, social media, communities, and email marketing, will build your personal brand. But there are many ways to accelerate the process even further.

It still begs the question: what are the benefits of building your personal brand?

First, remember that people buy from people, especially in B2B. The success of your SEO business depends on your ability to connect on a one-to-one basis with a decision-maker. It could be a solo business owner, startup founder, or CMO. The title doesn't matter.

What matters is that you're talking to another human being, and that's when personal branding comes into play. Ideally, you want your prospect to feel like they already "know" you before you even speak to them.

That's only possible when you develop your personal brand. If you do it right, the sales process is a thousand times easier. Memorize this sales and influence equation: **know + like + trust**. You develop all three parts of the equation by creating content and building your personal brand.

Newbies don't realize that fifty percent of your sales potential comes from what happens before prospects even get in touch with you.

I can tell you this from personal experience. Back in the day, I had to sell super hard when no one knew who I was. Meaning I had to try to convince prospect that I was competent and actually knew how to do SEO.

Fast forward to today – my sales process is insanely easy. I never have to convince someone to work with me. Instead, it's reversed. They must convince me they're a good fit for my SEO services. Not saying this to brag but to demonstrate why you need to start building your brand ASAP.

Think about it.

Do you think Dwayne "The Rock" Johnson needs to convince brands to work with him? Not a chance. The

Rock chooses who he wants to work with. He's in complete control. He owns the attention and authority and brands pay big money to rent it.

You can see this in action throughout daily life.

Brands hire celebrity spokespeople because of the undeniable equation of influence: know + like + trust. I could dedicate an entire book to personal branding, but here are some ways to build upon what you're already doing.

Work on Your Story

There are things that make you unique and relatable. But here's the important point: your stories must align with your target audience. Most people interested in SEO won't care about what you ate for breakfast. But they will care about how you got penalized by Google and recovered your lost rankings, for example.

Create a list about yourself. Don't hold anything back. Keep adding to the list as you remember past experiences.

Here's my "story" list for example:

My Story

Personal	Business

• Husband
• Father
• Dog owner
• Lakers fan
• MMA fan
• Learner
• Book reader
• Traveler
• Rubik's cube solver
• Chess player
	• Entrepreneur
	• Founder
	• Business Owner
	• Copywriter
	• SEO expert
	• Former black hat SEO
	    ○ PBNs
	    ○ Manual actions
	• SEO Coach
	• YouTuber

Start broad and then go deeper on each of these.

Keep in mind that you're not going to share everything about yourself online. Focus on what's relevant and then add some personal touches.

For example, Gary Vee does this very well. It's well-known that he's a New York Jets fan and wants to buy the team. He also shares his immigrant background and how it formed him as an entrepreneur. Ninety-nine percent of his content is focused on his core competencies like social media marketing, entrepreneurship, and personal development.

But when Gary shares something more personal, it always relates back to his core competencies.

The point is that people remember stories more than facts.

Start building your story database and share parts of it whenever you can.

Become A Guest Contributor

Guest posting is a powerful way to get brand exposure. In short, you'll write content for relevant websites and get a link back to yours. I recommend focusing on the industry you're targeting.

For example, if you're targeting plumbers, you should write content like "SEO for Plumbers: The Definitive Guide" and try to land placements on plumber-specific websites and SEO websites.

You can find these guest posting opportunities by searching Google:

- "plumber" + "write for us"
- "plumber" + "guest post"
- "SEO" + "write for us"

Then review the website's guest posting guidelines and pitch your ideas. I suggest pitching ideas and getting approval before creating the content.

Here's the template I often use:

Subject Line: Guest post ideas!

Hey [NAME],

My name is [YOUR NAME] and I'm the [POSITION] of [COMPANY].

I was wondering if you are still accepting guest posts on your blog.

I would love to get the opportunity to add value to your audience if you are.

Here are 3 ideas:

- [UNIQUE IDEA #1]

- [UNIQUE IDEA #2]

- [UNIQUE IDEA #3]

Let me know what you think, and thanks for your time!

Get Interviewed

You'll need some credibility to land interviews, but it's a powerful way to grow your authority. If you're new, the best thing to do is focus on podcasts with small audiences. You can score some quick wins and then leverage it to land interviews on bigger podcasts. The point is that you shouldn't expect to be on Joe Rogan. Push your ego to the side and focus on volume.

Here's how to find opportunities:

Use these search strings on Google like:

- "INFLUENCER NAME" + "interview"
- "NICHE" + "interview with"
- inurl:[keyword] inurl:podcast

Then use this template for your outreach:

Subject line: Podcast Guest Pitch: [TOPIC // EXPERTISE]

Hi [podcast host name],

I'm [name], and I'm a [POSITION] at [COMPANY]. I [What you do that's relevant to the podcast].

I really enjoyed the episode where you discussed [specific topic of the episode]. [Unique insight you gained from the episode].

I believe there is a gap in the conversation [unique value you can add]. I have a few ideas of what I could talk about on your podcast to help fix this. I could make an episode on any of these topics, or any other ideas you have that your audience would find interesting.

HEADLINE IDEA #1

HEADLINE IDEA #2

HEADLINE IDEA #3

[1-2 sentences explaining your credentials and why you're qualified to write about X].

So please let me know if you're accepting new guests because I would love to contribute. Thanks for your time!

Become an Interviewer

I call this the "Oprah Technique," and it allows you to get authority through osmosis. In other words, you'll gain authority status by associating yourself with other authority figures in the industry. Oprah, Joe Rogan, and Tim Ferriss, have all used this technique successfully.

The good news is that you don't need to build a massive podcast to get the benefits. Once again, stay focused on your target marketing.

1. Build a list of experts and influencers in your industry

Use search strings in Google like:

- Best [NICHE] podcasts (this one will help you identify interview opportunities)
- Top [NICHE] experts
- Best [NICHE] blogs
- Best [NICHE] experts to follow

2. Prioritize them based on authority

You shouldn't go for the top dogs in the industry right away. You need to build some credibility first because you can then use it as leverage. It's best to start with micro-influencers in the vertical and then pitch bigger experts once you've established your show.

3. Get prepared

Here's the bare minimum equipment/tools you'll need to start:

- **Microphone** - I use a Blue Yeti mic
- **Recording tool** - Zoom or riverside.fm
- **Audio editing tool** - iMovie is a free option for Mac users
- **Anchor** - Distribute content
- **Google** - Learn more about how to start a podcast

Then come prepared with well-thought-out questions. Most importantly, always make the interviewee the star of the show. Your job is to ask questions and listen.

HARO

HARO or Help a Reporter Out is a free service that gives you media coverage opportunities. They'll send you opportunities twice a day and you can respond to as many as you like. But submission does not equal inclusion. So it's a number's game.

You should try to respond to as many relevant opportunities as possible and expect only about 5-10% to land. But when they do land, they're super valuable. Not only will you get media coverage, but you'll also likely get a backlink to your website.

Just set a cadence of responding to one to three HARO requests per day. Keep in mind that longer doesn't equal better. For example, this one was accepted – it wasn't long, but it was unique:

> *Users should dictate the design and architecture of your website, not your opinion or subjective ideas about what constitutes good design. Your website should be designed to do one thing: get users to act. Every page on your website should have that intention.*
>
> *– Nathan Gotch, Founder, Gotch SEO*

Be Consistent

One intangible element of building a successful personal brand is consistency. You are the star of the show and people are watching you. You have to be consistent. There is no "end" to this game unless you want to sell your business.

You have to show up everyday and give value. Do that for an extended period of time, and people will begin to know, like, and trust you.

PART FOUR:

Close

"Most people think 'selling' is the same as 'talking'. But the most effective salespeople know that 'listening' is the most important part of their job." – Roy Bartell

---

Congrats! At this point, you've done all the hard work and attracted qualified traffic to your website. Now it's time to convert leads into clients.

Here's the process at a high level:

Discovery Call → Front-End Offer → Deliver Value → Full-Service SEO Proposal

The discovery call is where the process begins.

Conduct A Discovery Call

The discovery call is your first call with a potential client. It's critical for understanding their needs but also for vetting them. Remember, this is a partnership, and ideally you should only work with clients you want to work with. In addition, the discovery call allows you to "discover" warning signs of potentially toxic clients.

Of course, if you're new and need clients today, you might have to make some sacrifices. In other words, you might have to work with any client that comes your way. But, as your client base grows, you can start to be more selective about who you work with.

The first thing you need to do is, create a dedicated template for your discovery call questions. You'll make a copy of this template every time you book a discovery call booked on your calendar.

You might be thinking, *Why* do I need a script? Believe it or not, even the best salespeople use scripts. Scripts keep you focused on getting the answers you need to close a prospect if they're a good fit. Especially when you're having a rough day..

Note: Use the following questions as a guide. You may not need to ask all of them. Instead, use your best judgment based on the information the prospect gives you.

"How did you hear about us?"

You need this intel to see what traffic sources are generating the best leads. Then, once you start seeing a trend, you can invest more into whatever channel works best. For example, our leads often say "YouTube" or "Google," so we continue investing in those channels.

"What attracted you to our brand?"

In their own words, you want them to explain why they decided to book a call. The more you can get the client to sell themselves, the easier it will be for you. I don't always ask this question because they usually freely give this information.

For example, they might say, *"I was watching your YouTube video about on-page SEO and knew I needed your help."*

"Who else is part of this decision-making process?"

You must ask this question so you can gauge how long the sales cycle will be. For example, if you're talking to the decision-maker, you'll be able to close the deal faster. If not, you may be dealing with a bureaucratic process that involves several people which could take multiple calls to close.

"What's the company size?"

You can generally predict the company's revenue based on how many employees they have. While it's not a perfect predictor, it's pretty accurate. It's a sign of whether they can afford your services or not. For example, a one-person operation with only a few clients may not be a good fit for your largest monthly retainer.

"Are you targeting local or national customers?"

The total investment should change based on their answer. For example, my agency charges a minimum of $5,000/month for national and $2,500/month for local campaigns.

"How many locations are you servicing?"

You should charge more if they're trying to rank in many locations.

"Have you ever worked with an SEO company before?"

All the other questions are essential, but this one is critical. You need to get intel on their history of working with SEO companies. If they've never worked with one before, that's perfect. But it's always concerning to hear a company say they've worked with five to ten SEO companies in the past. Why?

Because it's a good sign they could be an agency-hopper that never commits to the outcome. In other words, they won't retain or give you a fair shot to deliver results. Once again, if you're new, take what you can get. But once you're more experienced, be careful.

The truth is that many SEO companies aren't great. Some do mediocre work or offer SEO as an upsell. So, it's not uncommon for a company to have worked with a few SEO companies.

But it's a red flag if they've worked with five or more and have nothing good to say about any of them.

The follow-up question is: *"How long have you worked with the current or previous SEO company?"* If they say less than six months, it's another red flag.

But if they say one year or more, you know they gave the

SEO company a fair shot.

"What are you hoping to accomplish in a new partnership?"

Once again, a question of selling themselves on what they want. The prospect's answers can help you craft your sales message within the proposal. Use their own words.

"What is your average customer lifetime value?"

Most businesses struggle to answer this question (which is hard to believe). However, it's critical to determine if you can generate an ROI.

For example, let's say the company's LTV (Lifetime Value) is only $15. And your retainer is $2,500/month. They would need 166 sales to break even. Compare that to a personal injury lawyer, who might have an LTV of $10,000. The personal injury lawyer would only need one sale to be profitable.

In short, it's usually easier to drive an ROI from the SEO campaign when the LTV is higher. Conversely, the only way a company with low LTV can generate an ROI from SEO is to generate tons of organic traffic.

From time to time, organic traffic simply isn't abundant enough in certain industries. So, it won't make sense for them to invest in SEO services (at least at the prices my agency offers). In fact, we often turn down prospects when we don't see a clear ROI path.

I'll share how you predict the ROI of an SEO campaign later on. But to do this calculation well, you'll need to get the LTV from the prospect upfront.

"What keywords would your ideal customers use to find your products or service?"

The goal is to get broad topics or seeds for deeper keyword research. It also allows you to analyze their industry and see if it's a good fit.

"Do you have a designer or developer who can make website changes for you?"

This intel will allow you to modify your SEO proposal based on their capabilities. For example, if they don't have developers or anyone who can make technical changes, you will have to do it.

Of course, this increases your fulfillment costs, so the SEO campaign investment should be higher.

On the opposite side, you'll act as an advisor if they do have developers. In short, you'll identify the technical SEO opportunities and then consult with their developers to get them fixed. It still takes time, but not as intensive as doing it yourself.

"Do you have someone who writes copy for your website?"

If the prospect has writers, you'll supply SEO content briefs and optimize the content. If they don't have writers, you'll have to manage the entire process from start to finish.

"When do you hope to get started?"

This question is to gauge how serious they are. If the prospect says they're not sure, don't expect them to close soon. If they say "ASAP," you're good to go.

"How do you measure success in an SEO campaign?"

Once again, we're getting them to tell us what they want. Then, you can use their language in your proposal.

"What are your long-term goals for your company?"

I always throw this one in because people love to talk about their companies (or themselves).

Here's a quote from How to Win Friends and Influence People by Dale Carnegie:

"To be interesting, be interested. Ask questions that other people will enjoy answering. Encourage them to talk about themselves and their accomplishments."

That's what you're doing here. Remember that "liking" is one of the critical persuasion levers. By showing interest in their company, your perceived status will climb.

Next Steps

So, you've asked all your questions. What do you do next? You need to outline the next steps based on their answers and how you're vibing with them.

If you've decided it's a good fit, you have two options: pitch a front-end offer (more on this in a second) or pitch full-service SEO.

A front-end, low-barrier-to-entry offer is the best option if you're new and trying to win new deals.

For example, an audit is a good option if the company has many internal resources but lacks SEO direction. You'll give them a roadmap to success, and they can execute on it. Often, they'll end up hiring you to execute it anyway.

But the key to a successful discovery call is to outline the next steps.

Here's what I often say:

Okay, awesome. So based on what you've shared, you need a focused SEO strategy for the next 1-2 years. Since you can execute technical changes and create content in-house, we can guide your team with our SEO audit and SEO recommendations. In short, we'll find every SEO opportunity on your site and in your industry.

Then we'll create a dedicated SEO recommendations document that categorizes all the opportunities from levels 1-3. Level 1 actions will deliver big SEO results. Level 3 actions are still essential but won't move the needle on their own. But as a cumulative and compounded action, it will help.

Then we'll also jump on a coaching call to discuss every SEO opportunity we've identified. We'll work through each one with your team so they can execute it correctly. Does that sound like something you'd be interested in?

If they agree, I'll say:

Okay, great! So, the next step is simple: I'll prepare a proposal for the audit, and then we'll need to jump on another quick call to discuss. It should only take a day or so. I'll email you once it's ready to go.

Keep in mind, you should only pitch an SEO audit if the business has the capability to execute on the recommendations. For example, if you're talking to a one-person law firm, then it makes more it makes more sense to skip the SEO proposal.

You need to use your best judgment based on their available resources. But if you're new, I would pitch a front-end offer most of the time.

Pitch a Front-End Offer

"90% of selling is conviction, and 10% is persuasion."
– Shiv Khera

I mentioned front-end offers in the previous section, but what does it mean?

In short, getting someone to commit to a lower-ticket product is easier than a higher-ticket one. That's because most people are risk averse. So by having an easier entry point with a front-end offer, you'll increase the odds of closing the sale.

But the front-end offer has deeper psychology.

When someone becomes a customer (they give you money), they're more likely to buy additional products from you. That's why McDonald's has the Dollar Menu. Not to make a fortune from it, but their goal is to keep coming back and have you spend more than you anticipated.

They're focused on the lifetime value of every customer. And that's what front-end offers can do.

It's essential when you're new to the agency game. You may not have well-refined sales skills when you're new, and you likely don't have an extensive SEO portfolio. Closing big deals with a three to six-month commitment will be tough. That's where the front-end offer comes in.

Before I show you the methods, here's what can happen if you're new and skip the front-end offer to pitch full-service SEO upfront:

Spend a week creating an SEO proposal just to get ghosted.

It happens to everyone, including me. But I can tell you from experience that it's never happened when I've closed a front-end offer. The reason is simple: **they are a customer at that point instead of a lead.** Customers act differently than people who haven't invested money.

Long, drawn-out sales cycle.

Closing some full-service SEO deals can take weeks (or even months), depending on the company's size. However, with front-end offers, you can close the deal within days or even sometimes right on the discovery call.

Pray that a client accepts your proposal based on random pricing.

How should you price your SEO services? Everyone is guessing and copying each other. But this becomes less relevant once you've demonstrated your value by delivering the front-end offer. Instead of the client wondering if they should work with you, you become the only option. All of sudden, they want to work with you.

Chasing clients out of desperation.

The client ghosts you, and now it's time to follow up out of desperation. It rarely works. If someone wants to work with you, they'll seek you out. Once again, the front-end offer nearly eliminates this issue.

The uneasy feeling that it may not work out.

Creating SEO proposals often feels like a shot in the dark. You work on it for days and then send it off with your fingers crossed. Sometimes it works, and other times you get ghosted. That's the bad news. However, soon I'll show you how to close about 50% of your proposals by doing the opposite of everyone else.

Agreeing to work with toxic clients.

This point is my biggest secret. In short, there are many toxic clients out there, but you can avoid them using the front-end offer—more on this in a second.

Here's a new way:

Stop creating proposals; start creating commitments.

When someone gives you money, they're committed to seeing it through. Also, people are more likely to invest in a one-time SEO solution when the relationship is new. Keep in mind once money has exchanged hands, your relationship has changed. Clients act differently than prospects. They're also a hundred times more likely to buy another product because they've transitioned out of the friend zone.

Make your competitors irrelevant.

The best part about the front-end offer is that you eliminate competition. The client is only thinking about you delivering the SEO audit. They're excited to see what you've done. As a result, you've already won the game of attention.

Deliver value and results in advance to prove your worth.

The beauty of the front-end offer is that you're proving the value you can add to their business. The goal is to blow the client's mind and make them realize they need your help. SEO audits are best for accomplishing this goal. I'll share what a strong SEO audit offer looks like.

No more long sales cycles.

Once you deliver the SEO audit, it's time to pitch full-service

SEO or consulting. This can be as easy as asking, "Would you like our help with this?" or a similar question. In some cases, the business will attempt to execute your SEO recommendations themselves. So, there might be a small gap between delivering the product and signing on. However, we've found that most clients want us to execute the plan for them. It just may take a few months to come full circle. So that's why you'll need to follow up.

Close ten times more SEO contracts without working any harder.

The client has already committed to you and invested money. If you do a killer job, there should be no other options. It's only a matter of budget and time.

Never chase clients down again.

When you deliver insane value, clients want to work with you. You don't have to convince or persuade them to become a client. Instead, you prove your worth by delivering exceptional work.

Only work with the best clients (through second-order vetting).

I coined this "second-order vetting" concept because I was sick of working with toxic clients. And that's the magic of the front-end offer. It gives you a preview of what it'll be like working with this client. If you're already not vibing well during this phase, then it's not a good sign for full-service SEO.

But the opposite is also true. If they're awesome during this phase, it's a very good sign for your business relationship. Generally, how it starts is how it ends.

The point is, you don't know how a client will be until money has exchanged hands. Of course, everyone is friendly on discovery calls. But you really find out how someone is after the first transaction.

Now that you understand the benefits of pitching front-end SEO offers, what should you pitch?

The complete SEO audit is my favorite front-end offer because it adds massive value.

Here's what's included in our SEO audits that we sell for $5,000 and up:

- SEO Audit
- Keyword Database
- SEO Competitor Analysis
- Technical SEO Audit
- SEO Content Audit
- Backlink Audit

- SEO Content Briefs (x10)
- Backlink Opportunities
- SEO Action Plan
- Video Explainer
- 1-on-1 SEO Coaching Session

This product delivers tons of value but can be harder to sell because of the higher investment. Keep in mind that the $5,000 audit is priced from my years of experience. In the beginning, I recommend starting lower and working your way up. Remember, the goal of the front-end offer is to turn leads into paying clients. If you can make a nice profit – great. But that's not the goal of the front-end offer.

You can also break the SEO audit down into micro-offers. So instead of offering the complete SEO audit, you can offer keyword research or an SEO content strategy. Since these are microservices, you can price them lower and lower the barrier to entry.

Here are some micro-SEO services that you can offer on the front end:

- Keyword Research
- SEO Competitor Analysis
- Technical Audit
- Content Audit
- SEO Content Strategy (3, 6, or 12 months)
- Backlink Audit

- Backlink Acquisition Plan
- Local SEO Audit
- Google Business Profile Creation + Optimization
- Competitor Gap Analysis
- Ranking Diagnosis

Test many different front-end offers and see which one converts best. Once you close a deal, the process is as follows:

Create A Statement of Work (SOW)

An SOW is a simple one-page document outlining all the agreement's terms and conditions. Never start without a signature.

Send the Invoice

Warning: do not start any work until they've paid the invoice. Never work for free.

Get Tool Access

You'll need access to Google Analytics and Google Search Console if you're conducting an SEO audit. If you're doing a micro front-end offer, you may not need access.

Deliver Massive Value

All you need to do now is deliver tremendous value to the client. I recommend completing all the deliverables and then jumping on a call with them to discuss with the client. From there, you can transition into selling a full-service SEO solution. If the client agrees to move forward, then it's time for an SEO proposal.

Create an SEO Proposal

> *"I fear not the man who has practiced 10,000 kicks once, but I fear the man who has practiced one kick 10,000 times." – Bruce Lee*

An SEO proposal is a presentation, webpage, or document explaining why the client should work with you, all the SEO opportunities, and what you can offer.

Once you agree that a proposal is the next best step, you must follow a simple process.

After the discovery call, wait a day and then send an email letting them know the proposal is ready. Here's the exact template I use:

Hey Joe, your SEO proposal is ready to go! Please go here to book a call to discuss. Thanks!

Now here's the key: **DO NOT** send the proposal. Even if they ask.

I don't let them see the proposal until they're on the call. There are a few reasons for this.

First, it prevents price shoppers who are looking for the cheapest deal they can find. Second, I do something that's pretty tricky but helps to prevent time wasters. So when I send the "SEO proposal is ready" email, I haven't even started the proposal yet. You might be thinking, Sounds crazy, right?

Here's the deal: you don't want to invest time into a custom proposal until they've committed to a call. As you'll see in a second, my process for developing SEO proposals is intense. The last thing you want to do is build this proposal and then get ghosted.

Second, it gives you a shot at actually winning the business. You're going to walk through each part of the proposal in a logical order. If you were to send the prospect the proposal via email, they would quickly scroll down to the pricing section.

Price is relative. If they see a big number, they'll be resistant. But it's a different story if the prospect sees the number after you explain each part of the process and use some persuasion techniques.

Once you book the call, create the proposal and then you'll present it on a Zoom or Google Meet call. Also, make sure your calendar blocks out the day when you send the booking email. If you haven't created the proposal yet, obviously you don't want them to book on the same day.

Create Your SEO Proposal

Now it's time to learn how to create SEO proposals that get 50% close rates. I will warn you, though, these proposals are not easy to create. Therefore, you must be only creating proposals for qualified prospects. When you see the process, you'll understand why.

First, how should you create your SEO proposal? When I first started, I would create it on a Google Doc and then export it as a PDF. I don't recommend this option, though. Instead, I recommend using an affordable design tool like Canva or your website.

Canva has hundreds of proposal templates you can use. It's worth every penny. Think of Canva as your graphic designer.

The second option is to use your website and Canva. In this scenario, I'll create a dedicated page on our website for the client (example: gotchseo.com/clients-brand-name/). This is unique and will help you stand out.

In short, we've created a basic template on our site and filled it with details specific to the prospective client—more on this in a second.

Now there are only two formats you can use for SEO proposals. A traditional page that scrolls or a deck (Google

Slides, PowerPoint, or even Canva). I've seen no difference in conversion rates based on the format. So, I recommend testing to find what works best for you.

The #1 Key to Successful SEO Proposals

The only way you can get 50% close rates on your proposals is to A) make sure you're presenting to the correct prospects and B) make sure your proposal is highly personalized. Most newbies fail with point B including myself when I was new.

Why? Because I wanted to get as many SEO proposals out there as possible. As a result, all my SEO proposals were pretty much the same. Or, in other words, cookie-cutter. It still worked, but I doubled my sales conversion rate when I started to personalize.

You want the client to feel special and know that you took the time to analyze their situation like a real professional would. It doesn't mean you're always going to win the deal. But when it comes to business, it's always better to know that you did everything you could to earn that client. You'll win some and lose some.

The best way to critique yourself is by measuring the effort you put into your proposals. Even if you don't get the deal,, you can still feel satisfied knowing you did what you could. Leave it all out on the field.

Now it's time to show you the most important sections of your proposal. Use these as inspiration but you don't need to do it exactly like I do. Find what works for you and run with it.

Section 1: Executive Summary

The first section of your proposal is what's called an "Executive Summary." Don't worry about the corporate jargon. It's a simple three to four sentence summary of prospective clients' situations and how you will help them.

This section is critical because it will show how much you paid attention in the discovery call. You must use the discovery call template and take detailed notes. I use the notes from the discovery call to craft the executive summary. Try to use your client's words in the summary.

Here's an example:

ABC Corp wants more qualified leads from Google that convert into high-paying patients without having to pay for ads. In this SEO proposal I'll show you how we're going to 10x ABC Corp's organic traffic, leads, and patients using Google.

Section 2: SEO Opportunities

You will present several (not all) of the current SEO opportunities. Typically, I'll present anywhere between three to seven opportunities. Keep in mind that I'm showing the opportunity, but I'm giving them a blueprint for taking advantage of it. That's the point of hiring us.

What I like to do is do a basic SEO audit to find common opportunities.

1. Google PageSpeed Insights

Run the prospect's site through this tool and take a screenshot if the scores are low.

2. Siteliner

Siteliner will show you duplicate content on a website and broken links.

Once again, take a screenshot if there's excessive duplicate content (20%+).

3. Ahrefs

Always run the site through Ahrefs to look for two different opportunities. First, go to "Organic Keywords" and click "Positions." Next, click the "Positions" dropdown and enter "#2-#15."

These keywords are what I like to call "low-hanging fruits." Finding low-hanging fruit keywords should be the focus at the beginning of an SEO campaign. They only need a slight push to generate more organic traffic. Take a screenshot of these opportunities.

The second way to find opportunities with Ahrefs is to go to the Site Explorer, enter the target domain, and click on Overview 2.0. You'll then see their DR (Domain Rating), which is how strong their website is from a backlink perspective. If it's below 30, then there's room to improve.

4. Screaming Frog SEO Spider

Screaming Frog is the most technical part of this process, but it can reveal many SEO opportunities. Download Screaming Frog and enter the prospect's domain. I recommend exporting the report and putting it into a Google Sheet because it's easier to manage.

Once it's in a Google Sheet, freeze the top row, and add a filter.

Look under the **Content Type** column, click the filter, and deselect everything except for **text/html**.

Now go to the **Indexability** column and select **Indexable**.

The first place to look for opportunities is under the **Word**

Count. Filter from A-Z to see pages with low word counts. Any pages with less than 400 words fall under the **Thin Content** category.

amphtml Lin	Size (bytes)	Word Count	Text Ratio	Crawl Depth	Link
	69999	29	0.3	3	
	79135	77	0.644	1	
	77699	123	1.108	2	
	79786	148	1.173	3	
	81713	152	1.338	5	
	80916	152	1.267	5	
	81646	153	1.265	10	
	80589	154	1.313	7	
	80907	155	1.2	10	
	80468		1.248	2	

Next, look at the **Crawl Depth** column and sort from Z-A. Any pages more than three clicks deep into the site architecture have Poor Crawl Depth. **Poor crawl depth** makes it difficult for Google to crawl, index, and rank those pages. So, you need to push those pages further up the architecture if you want them to perform better.

Word Count	Text Ratio	Crawl Depth	Link Score
165	1.318	18	
162	1.274	17	
165	1.296	17	
163	1.251	16	
164	1.289	16	
163	1.257	15	
166	1.288	15	
165	1.333	14	

The next column to look at is **Unique Inlinks**. Sort from A-Z, and you'll see what pages have a small number of internal links.

Inlinks	Unique Inlinks	Unique JS In	0
2	2	0	
8	3	0	
8	3	0	
8	3	0	
8	3	0	
8	3	0	
8	3	0	

We classify pages with less than three internal links as having poor internal link coverage. In short, you need to find more internal linking opportunities on the website. Otherwise, it's a sign that you need to create more topically relevant content to support those under-linked assets.

Now, how do you present these opportunities in the proposal? Here's a simple format (plus some examples):

First, always positively present the opportunity. For example, don't say, *"Your Crawl Depth Sucks."* Instead, say, *"Optimize Crawl Depth."*

Next, write a brief explanation of why the opportunity is vital for SEO performance. Once you get better, you may not need descriptions, but in the beginning, I recommend it.

Then, highlight the opportunity on the screenshot you took using a red box or red arrow.

To review, write about the opportunity using positive language, describe why it's crucial for SEO, and add a visual representation of the opportunity.

You'll then organize the list of opportunities into a numbered list.

In the presentation, go through each opportunity and briefly discuss why they're essential.

Section 3: Process + Timeline

Now it's time to give a high-level overview of your SEO process. Don't be afraid to use lots of detail here. There is a danger of being too simple because other SEO companies will put all kinds of fluff and jargon into their proposals.

Unfortunately, most businesses fall for these tactics because they "don't know what they don't know."

It's best to list each part of your process and the timeline.

For example, "Month 1 - Build A Keyword Database." Then, explain (with visuals). The key is to focus on visuals, not big blocks of text. You may need some text to keep you on track if you're new.

But, as your experience grows, the visuals prompt you, and you'll know what to say.

Section 4: Case Studies / Results

It doesn't matter how much value you add; prospective clients will still put the most weight on results. In particular, they'll want to see results from other businesses preferably in their industry.

Sometimes this isn't possible in the beginning. So having *any* results is still valuable.

What I like to do is a "before and after" case study. I'll add three case studies to this section titled something like "147% More Organic Search Traffic." Then I'll explain where this client was when they started with us (the before). Next, I'll show the actions we took. Lastly, I'll show the results of those actions (the after).

If you don't have any clients yet, rank any website (friends, family members, your own site) and use it as your own personal case study. Get creative – where there's a will, there's always a way.

This gives prospective clients a sneak peek into how you work. I recommend at least three case studies, and then you can follow that up with screenshots of the results.

More is always better.

Section 5: Investment

It's time to present the investment. Notice I'm saying "investment," not "price" or "cost." Words matter. Always use "investment" when speaking about your SEO services.

This isn't some tricky persuasion tactic. It's the truth. When you put a dollar in and expect two dollars back, that's an investment. That's how SEO works when you get results. You invest in the campaign, which drives more organic traffic, leads, sales, and revenue.

It's similar to investing in stocks since the ROI doesn't happen overnight. If you invest $10,000 into the S&P 500, it won't become $20,000 tomorrow. But, in ten to twenty years, there's a good chance it will have grown.

SEO doesn't take that long, but the concept is still the same. If a company invests $5,000/month into SEO and then makes $100,000/month more revenue, it's a good investment. Your goal as an SEO company is to generate an ROI for your clients. If you do, it's a no-brainer that they'll keep working with you.

Next, I recommend presenting your investment in three tiers, which leverages price anchoring. You'll need to test which deliverables should be in each tier. But I recommend getting granular with the deliverables.

For my agency, the most significant difference between our tiers is in the on-page SEO, content creation, and link-building deliverables. For example, the larger investment gets a higher volume while the lower ones get less.

Section 6: Next Steps

Always assume the close unless told otherwise. Then, it's time to outline the next steps.

For example, I have a dedicated "Next Steps" section. It says:

1. Pick a package.

2. Send a Statement of Work (SOW) and the first invoice.

3. Once it's signed, we'll schedule a kickoff call.

4. Get started!

So you could say something like: "Now if you decide to move forward John, here are the next steps... (go through each step). Where would you like to go from here?"

I cannot stress this enough. Always assume you've won the business until you hear a clear "no." It will show confidence and conviction.

Bonus Step: Proactively Offer Referrals

While this won't be possible when you're new, it's powerful when you have more experience. Keep a record of your best clients and ask them if they can be your referrals. If so, you can send a prospective client three referrals they can call on.

Of course, most won't take you up on the offer. But it's the action and transparency that are so powerful.

Last Word on SEO Proposals

Use parts of my process and test to see what works best for you. The most important part of your SEO proposal is personalization. It needs to be clear to the prospective client that you understand their business and unique SEO situation. Don't take shortcuts when creating proposals for qualified prospects. The better your proposal, the easier it will be to close.

Sales Techniques

"Start working with your prospects as if they've already hired you." — Jill Konrath.

Fact: Learning how to sell is the most valuable skill you can learn as an entrepreneur. It's the key to achieving your potential. Do not take it lightly.

But how do you get better at selling? First, use the following methods covered in this chapter. Second, put in your reps.

Yes, there are some rare savants who could sell a ketchup popsicle to a woman in white gloves. But for 99% of people, you'll need to work hard on your sales skills. I recommend using a script and recording your sales calls (with prospect approval) so you can review your performance, similar to how athletes review tape from their games. Then try to be a little better with each call. There's always room to improve your delivery, cadence, and how you handle objections.

Here are some techniques to use:

Set up the rules so you always win

One of the biggest challenges salespeople face is how they deal with rejection. Truth be told, the vast majority of sales calls I've done end without a sale. So will yours. But if getting a "yes" is the only way you measure your sales success, you'll end up feeling miserable most of the time.

The good news is that you can change the rules to make it a lot easier to win the game of sales. And it has everything to do with your mindset.

Here's the secret: Instead of thinking "yes = success" and "no = failure", I recommend changing your thought process to "making an offer = success" and focus on making more offers.

It sounds deceptively simple but if you truly adopt this mindset, you'll win on every sales call because your goal is to make an offer, not close them. Like the old saying goes, "You can lead a horse to water, but you can't make it drink." Similarly, you can't force a prospect to do anything. You can make them an offer, but ultimately it's their decision.

So the sooner you focus on what you can control (making offers) and let go of what's outside of your control (getting a "yes"), the sooner you'll feel a thousand times better about your sales process. And when you get really good at this, getting a "yes" shouldn't feel much different than making the offer in the first place.

Always focus on making more money/revenue growth

Don't get into the weeds with geeky SEO terminology and strategy – talk about the outcome. Remember, the client only cares about their Return on Investment (ROI). In other words, if they invest $1, will they get $2 (or more) back? Focus on that.

Have conviction, but don't over-promise

Believing in what you're selling is critical. But you also have to avoid overpromising what you can deliver. SEO is an unpredictable beast sometimes, and you don't want to put yourself in a difficult situation because you've made promises you can't keep..

Therefore, I recommend under promising and over delivering when it comes to SEO. While there are some SEOs who guarantee results, it's mostly because they're desperate for sales. The truth is, established agency owners know that you don't need to guarantee results to close deals.

Put it in a different context. Imagine if an investment firm guaranteed 20% returns every year in the stock market. You'd probably be skeptical and think it's some kind of Bernie Madoff situation. It's the same with SEO. Although SEO can be somewhat predictable by following best practices and having patience, there are still many factors outside of our control.

To be more specific, we don't control what Google does. They can change their algorithm with a snap of their fingers and rock the SEO world overnight. Don't worry, it's not as volatile as it sounds. I've been doing SEO since 2011, and I have been through many algorithm cycles. The key point is to not over-promise because it will wreck your reputation if you can't deliver.

As Warren Buffett says, *"It takes twenty years to build a reputation and five minutes to ruin it. If you think about that, you'll do things differently."*

The good news is that under promising is a powerful tool for sales and actually sets you up for success. From a sales perspective, it makes you look more trustworthy by not over-promising. And from a fulfillment perspective, it gives you much more flexibility to deliver results in a realistic timeframe. So be confidently humble, it's better all around.

Always speak in terms of honest data (not opinion or theory)

Many SEO "gurus" out there base their SEO guidance on their own unproven theories or what they've heard from someone else. Big mistake. You need to be prepared when a client asks the infamous question: "How much traffic will we get?"

Most people focusing on closing the sale will try to predict the outcome based on what sounds good or their super-optimistic opinion—a big mistake. Instead, you need to use data to project the possible outcome.

For example: *"We'll have a better idea of the potential traffic once we conduct the keyword research. First, we'll see the total available search volume in your industry, and then we'll estimate how much traffic you'll get based on ranking positions and organic CTR."*

The best salespeople I know are radically honest and transparent with their prospects and customers. In other words, they don't sound or act like salespeople. Let that sink in.

Listen first, ask questions second

Great salespeople are great listeners. You should practice active listening during your sales calls by taking notes and asking questions to get more information and clarify what you're being told. Review the questions I go over in the previous "Conduct a Discovery Call" section.

An easy way to remember this is with the acronym LART:

Listen – Take notes on every sales call and resist the temptation to interrupt your prospect. You want them doing most of the talking.

Acknowledge – By paraphrasing or restating what they've told you, it shows that you're actually listening to them and understand what they're telling you. For example, after they've answered your Discovery Call questions, you could say, "So let me just make sure I understand you correctly John..." and then summarize their situation, issues, and challenges.

Respond – Give your prospects the opportunity to ask you any final questions or voice any concerns or objections they may have. Respond with empathy and reassure them how you can solve their problems. Selling isn't about convincing – it's all about assuring. Assuring your prospect that you can make their life better if they invest in your services.

Transition – Use a simple statement or question to transition into the close. For example, I like to inject "implied closes" throughout the call such as "Once we start the campaign, we'll conduct extensive keyword research on all opportunities in your vertical."

Then at the end of your presentation, you can ask "So when would you like to get started, John?" or if you prefer to be less aggressive, "Where would you like to go from here?" Your only job is to nail down when that next step (if there is to be one) will happen. Put it on the calendar (ideally, it's a scheduled appointment with the client).

Follow Up

"Persistence, persistence, persistence. I'm surprised how few entrepreneurs follow up." – Mark Suster

News flash: Most prospective clients aren't going to sign up right away. Cue the follow-up. According to Better Proposals, 80% of sales come after the fifth to twelfth contact. Doesn't matter what the real number is, persistence is the name of the game.

You don't have to be annoying or pushy. Instead, just use a system that makes it repeatable.

Before I show you the cadence of following up, here are some basic principles to abide by:

1. Keep it simple

Focus on one thing at a time and keep it short.

2. Focus on them

How can you serve them? What value can you add to make the process easier, better, faster, etc?

3. Ask open-ended questions

Open-ended questions leave open loops in the prospect's

mind because they normally can't be answered with a simple "yes" or "no". Use them throughout the follow-up process.

4. Be professional

Some people get offended when prospects ghost them. Get used to it! Ghosting is a common business practice because it's easier than saying no. Don't get offended and take it personally. Stay the course, but be professional and respectful of other people's time.

5. Don't act desperate

There's a difference between persistence and desperation. Adhere to your follow-up cadence, but don't ever look desperate. Focus on adding value every email.

Now that you know some basic principles, here's an example of a simple follow-up process:

Post-Proposal Follow-Up Cadence

Day 1

This is one day after you've sent the proposal or SOW. Keep it simple here. I recommend something like this:

Hey Joe, we're having some issues with our email deliverability. Did you receive the docs I sent yesterday?

The goal of this email is to stay top-of-mind without being pushy. You have to remember that you don't always lose SEO contracts because of competitors. Sometimes you lose them because of inaction. The company wants SEO, but they need more nurturing.

Day 7

If you still haven't received a response, try something like this:

> Hey Joe, hope your week has been going well and just wanted to circle back with you regarding the SEO proposal I sent on April 15th.
>
> I know you were hoping to respond by (X day or date e.g. Tuesday or April 25th) but let me know if you have any additional questions and I'll get back to you ASAP.

Once again, think about how you can add value.

Day 14

> Hey Joe, just wanted to touch base regarding the SEO proposal I sent you. We still have a few spots left on our roster, but it looks like we'll be booked up soon. Do you still want in?

At this point, I've injected some subtle urgency and scarcity into the mix. You should try to pull a different persuasion lever with every follow-up email.

Day 21

Hey Joe, check this out:

We just {insert relevant client result or outcome}. This is what you can expect when we work together. Speaking of which, when would you like to get started?

You're stacking on the social proof here and implying the close.

Day 28

If you haven't received a response at this point, it's time for the breakup email. You'll be shocked how well this works.

Here's what to send:

{FIRST NAME},

Since I haven't heard from you, I assume you've gone in a different direction or your priorities have changed since we spoke.

Feel free to reach out if we can help you in the future.

Best,

{YOUR NAME}

Here's a real response from a prospect using this email:

"Hi Nathan,

Actually, I am still considering. I have signed a contract to handle of all my PPC and other online ads, and I want to see where we are after that is in full swing. Then I will decide if I need to invest even more each month for SEO. I still may hire you to do a deep dive analysis but am waiting to see the results in our lead flow from significantly increasing our ad spend and using new strategies.

Thanks and don't write me off just yet. :)"

Believe it or not, this client ended up investing $5,000 for an SEO audit. Don't underestimate the power of following up.

But what happens when you send the breakup email and still don't get a response? It's time to pay them a visit in person.

Kidding. You'll move the prospect to your regular broadcast list and end your personalized one-on-one follow up.

Onboarding

"We see our customers as invited guests to a party, and we are the hosts. It's our job every day to make every important aspect of the customer experience a little bit better." – Jeff Bezos

---

So, you've landed your first SEO client – congrats! Now what? Simply follow this process to deliver the best possible client experience imaginable.

1. Create A Statement of Work (SOW)

I've mentioned an SOW for front-end offers, but you'll also use it for full-service SEO.

It's a simple one-page document that outlines the terms of the engagement like so:

Statement of Work

This statement of work is between [YOU] and [CLIENT].

Effective date: Enter the date that the engagement will begin. E.g. *"This SOW is effective as of [MONTH] [DAY], [YEAR]."*

Project scope: Write a one to two-sentence description of what you'll be doing for the project. E.g. *"Monthly link building + SEO advising for on-page SEO and SEO content."*

Project objectives: Clarify what the goals and objectives are for the campaign (be specific). E.g. *"This project aims to identify SEO opportunities that can help [COMPANY NAME OR WEBSITE] increase its organic search traffic by growing website authority, optimizing existing content, and creating new SEO-driven content. This will be achieved by identifying the right opportunities and coaching [COMPANY]'s team through the implementation process."*

Location: It might sound odd, but you should clarify where the work will take place. E.g. *"All work and communication will occur digitally and remotely."*

Project deliverables: Get specific about the deliverables your client can expect on a monthly basis. E.g. *"Acquire 10-12 editorial backlinks, perform on-page SEO (or provide guidance) for (x10) pages, and create (x2) SEO content briefs every month."*

Schedules: Reiterate when the deliverables will be completed. E.g. *"Deliverables will be completed every month."*

Requirements: List what you will need access to for deliverable completion. E.g. *"We will need 'Viewer' access for Google Analytics & Google Search Console. Also 'Editor' access for CMS to make on-page SEO changes. We can also send the changes and you can implement them in-house."*

Payments: Establish the payment terms. Reminder: You should always be paid upfront for your work. E.g. *"A payment of $7,500 will be paid on the 1st of every month."*

Guarantees: You can't guarantee SEO results, just like you can't guarantee investment returns. Make it clear. E.g. *"Gotch SEO, LLC does not guarantee results."*

Disclaimer: Protect your business from legal issues with a disclaimer. E.g. *"Gotch SEO, LLC is not responsible/liable for loss of rankings, traffic, or revenue as a result of our recommendations and/or work."*

Refunds: Your fees should be non-refundable because you can't take back time and effort. Make it clear. E.g. *"All fees are non-refundable."*

[COMPANY NAME OR WEBSITE]	[YOUR COMPANY]
Signature: _____	Signature: _____
Printed Name: _____	Printed Name: _____
Title: _____	Title: _____
Date: _____	Date: _____

At my agency, we have the SOW template as a Google Doc and make a copy each time we land a new client. Then, we personalize it, and export it as a PDF. This PDF is then uploaded to DocuSign, so you can create signature fields. You can use whatever signature software you want, but this makes it much easier while giving you a more professional appearance.

Send the official SOW to the client and wait for the signature. If you don't get a signature within a week, follow up and make sure they received it.

Important: Don't do any work until this document is signed!

2. Send an Invoice with Stripe

You can bill however you please, but Stripe makes life easier. You simply add the client as a customer in Stripe and then send them an invoice.

Or you can put them on a recurring subscription that bills on the 1st or 15th of every month – this is what I do and recommend you do the same.

3. Conduct A Campaign Kickoff Call

A kickoff call is critical for the campaign to get off the ground and to establish expectations. Keep it simple and short. We schedule a Zoom call and use a Google Slides presentation to hit all the key points.

First, who's going to be the point of contact? In the early stages of your agency, that'll be you. Make that clear at the onset:

Your SEO Manager

Nathan Gotch

SEO Manager

nathan@gotchseo.com

GOTCH SEO

Second, establish a rough timeline of deliverables:

Timeline

Months 1-3

- Keyword Research, Competitor Analysis, Technical SEO, On-Page SEO, & SEO Content Creation

Months 3 +

- Link Building, Optimizing Existing Pages on Website, and New SEO Content

GOTCH SEO

Next, emphasize the Key Performance Indicators (KPIs). This is critical for establishing expectations. Your job as an SEO expert is not to drive leads, sales, or revenue. Those are the outcomes of your work. And yes, keyword selection does influence conversion rates. But in most cases, the product offerings, CRO (Conversion Rate Optimization), UX (User Experience), copywriting, and various other factors influence conversions much more.

Make it clear how your success as an SEO will be measured at the onset so there's no confusion:

Key Performance Indicators (KPIs)

1. Individual keyword rankings
2. Total organic keyword growth
3. Organic search traffic

GOTCH SEO

Now you need to establish both short and long-term goals for the campaign. Once again, the goal is to set realistic expectations.

Our Two Big Goals for You

Short-Term Goal: Build a Strong Foundation for Future SEO Performance.

Long-Term Goal: More Traffic, Leads, and Customers from Organic Search.

GOTCH SEO

Next, get more clarification about critical parts of delivering the service. For example, you should have a discussion about their products and services. You'll then be able to use these as seeds for keyword research. You'll need to confirm their available resources from a copywriting and development perspective.

You'll have gathered much of this information during the discovery phase, but it's important to get clarification again because it dictates how you'll fulfill the service.

Questions for You

1. What are some topics / broad keywords that your ideal customers might use to look for solutions like yours?

2. Do you have a subject matter expert available who can write or fact check content?

3. Do you have someone in-house (or external) who makes technical changes to your website?

GOTCH SEO

Next, explain what they need to do on their end so you can do your work:

What We Need From You

1. Google Analytics Access
2. Google Search Console Access

Give view access to support@gotchseo.com

GOTCH SEO

Then set a campaign launch date so everyone's on the same page:

Your SEO Campaign Goes Live on...
MONTH DAY, YEAR

GOTCH SEO

Lastly, finish up the kickoff call with some basic Q&A:

Questions?

GOTCH SEO

Don't overthink the kickoff call. Keep it short and sweet. The main goals of the kickoff call are to build rapport and trust with the client. Yes, it's also to hand the campaign from the sales team to the accounts team and to gather important information. But in reality, the kickoff call is another trust-building exercise.

Remember, retaining your clients isn't just about getting results. You need to manage the account and ensure that the client's experience is stellar.

4. Get Tool Access

You'll need access to Google Analytics, Google Search Console, and the client's Content Management System

(CMS) to conduct a proper SEO campaign.

I recommend creating a simple SOP (Standard Operating Procedure) that you send to every new client.

PART FIVE:

Retain

"To keep a customer demands as much skill as to win one."
– American Proverb

Now that you've onboarded your client, it's time to fulfill the work. What I'm about to show you is the perfect SEO fulfillment team. Think of this structure as your future goal. In reality, you'll fulfill all of these roles in the beginning.

But as you grow, you should slowly systemize and delegate these roles to other people.

There are three critical parts of successful fulfillment:

1. Account Management

The Account Manager (AM) is one hundred percent responsible for making sure the client is happy. They relay information from the client to the team executing the work. They also update the client on work that's been completed or currently in progress and report on KPIs.

In short, the account manager acts as the middleman between the client and the SEO team doing the work.

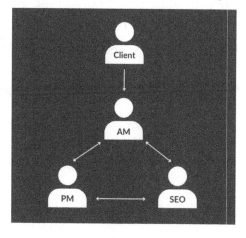

The reason why you need this role is because being a successful account manager requires a different skill set than someone who is doing technical work like SEO.

Account managers need strong soft skills for communicating with clients and weathering all storms.

Client Experience

Your team must have a clear cadence of communication to ensure that the client is happy. Here's the framework I recommend for SEO campaigns:

Weekly Touchpoints

Don't overthink this. Just send a quick email to your client every week sharing the work you've done or some noteworthy result you've achieved. You never want the client guessing what you're doing. Be proactive. I suggest sharing a Google sheet with your client containing 2 tabs: one for listing all "Completed" actions and one for listing "Next" actions that are currently in progress or in the pipeline.

Bottom line: You never want the client guessing what you're doing. Be proactive.

Here's a simple template you can use:

Subject Line: SEO update (week of MONTH/DAY/YEAR)

Hey {NAME},

Here's a quick weekly update on your SEO campaign:

What we completed (click here to see "Completed" tab)

1.

2.

3.

What we're working on (click here to "Next" tab)

1.

2.

3.

Results (click here to Semrush dashboard)

1.

2.

3.

Let me know if you have any questions, thanks!

Monthly Report

The monthly report is a roundup of all the work you've completed, what's next, and the results. Here's the template that we use:

Subject Line: SEO report for {MONTH} {YEAR}

Hey {NAME},

Here's your SEO report for {MONTH}, {YEAR}:

What we did this month:

1.

2.

3.

Click here to see the "Completed Actions" tab for more details.

What we're doing next month:

1.

2.

3.

Click here to see the "Next Actions" tab for more details.

Results:

1.

2.

3.

Review your Semrush KPI dashboard for more details.

Let me know if you have any questions, thanks!

2. Project Management

The Project Manager (PM) is responsible for assigning work and making sure deadlines are met. They are not account managers and they do not execute SEO work.

Their number-one goal is making sure the workflow is smooth, and they must manage the workload of the team. They'll work directly with the AM and SEO team to deliver services on time and on budget. Here's an example weekly report template that the PM sends to the AM:

Subject Line: Weekly Update

Hey Nathan,

Here's my update for the week:

What did you do this week?

- Optimized (x5) pages for ABC Corp.

- Delegated (x3) writing assignments for ABC Corp.

- Sent end-of-the-month reports to clients.

- Had (x3) meetings with clients.

What's your plan for next week?

- Optimize (x5) pages for Billy's Tacos.

- Create (x10) SEO content briefs for ABC Corp.

- Conduct keyword research for the Tesla campaign.

Where are you blocked?

- We need ABC Corp to optimize for Core Web Vitals, but we're struggling to get it in their development pipeline. We made the recommendation 45 days ago and still no progress.

Don't underestimate how important these weekly reports are. They keep everyone accountable and on the same page.

3. SEO Execution

A perfect SEO team is composed of an SEO director, SEO specialist, copywriter, graphic designer, and developer. The SEO director is responsible for developing the SEO strategy for each client on a monthly basis. They then assign the execution of the strategy to the SEO specialist. The SEO specialist reports to the SEO director. The SEO director will also act as quality control for all the SEO work. Keep in mind, you don't need this much complexity in the beginning. In fact, you'll be occupying all these roles. But as you grow, you'll need to get help.

Now that you know what a strong fulfillment and SEO team looks like, it's time to tackle the SEO execution itself.

SEO 101

"If you're not meeting your visitors' needs, it doesn't matter how 'optimized' your site is." – Stoney deGeyter

Most of this book has focused on the business side of SEO. Now it's time to cover some basics on how to do the actual SEO work.

Earlier in this book, you learned that 90.63% of web pages get zero organic search traffic from Google (Ahrefs, 2020). So the question is, why do so many people fail at SEO?

Well, there are three simple reasons:

1. They're in love with tactics

I used to play Mortal Kombat when I was younger, and I would infuriate my friend by using the same Johnny Cage move over and over.

He couldn't stop it. But guess what? It was nothing more than a tactic. I wasn't good at the game. So, I just found a loophole and exploited it.

I sacrificed long-term skill-building for short-term gains. And that's what people do in SEO. They find a tactic and think it'll change the game for them. Sometimes it does, but most of the time, it's short-lived. Then they're right back where they started.

Or they continue seeking the next big guru tactic that'll save their SEO like a hamster on a wheel.

2. They're doing guesSEO

Some tactics may work, but newbies usually don't know why. They forget that correlation isn't causation. In other words, sometimes a rookie will think a specific SEO tactic is the sole reason for some ranking success, when in reality it did nothing

But because they believe it did, they keep doing it (the wrong thing), which leads to more confusion. They have no systems and no strategy. They're just throwing stuff at the wall and hoping it works.

3. They pray instead of know

What if Lebron James only hoped and prayed that he played well in basketball? It may have some benefit, but Lebron plays well because he knows he'll play well. How?

Because he's built muscle memory from thousands of hours of practice. Lebron is probably surprised when he doesn't play well because that would be an anomaly.

Like basketball, SEO is a skill. The more you do it (the right way), the more muscle memory you build. Successful SEOs don't hope or pray for results. Instead, they execute and wait for the results they know are coming.

To review, here's the equation for consistent SEO failure:

Tactics + GuesSEO + Prayer = Random, Unpredictable SEO Results

That's the bad news. The good news is that there's a better and easier way to succeed with SEO.

Let me walk you through the SEO formula (that works).

First of all, elite SEO pros don't simply hope for results or rely on other people's opinions. Instead, they are architects of an SEO system that's been refined and optimized over time. If you do it right, the system should be effective for someone at any skill level. In other words, you shouldn't have to depend on self-proclaimed SEO gurus to achieve rankings.

You'll be able to integrate anyone into the system and still get SEO results (even if they've never done SEO before). What does a sound SEO system look like?

Well, the easiest thing to do is walk you through the SEO system I've built and optimized for the last ten years. It's worked on the hundreds of SEO campaigns I've led and for literally thousands of successful SEO pros that are using it today.

Step #1 - Find, Qualify, and Prioritize Keywords

Keywords are the foundation of every successful SEO campaign. But here's the truth: Anyone can find keywords. The real skill comes from knowing what keywords to target. That's when knowing how to qualify and prioritize keywords comes into play.

But let's start with some simple ways to find keywords for your industry.

1. Start with your website

The best way to start is with keywords that are currently performing well for you. These keywords are the best because Google is already signaling that you're doing something right to show up organically.

Now go to Ahrefs, enter your domain into the Site Explorer, go to **Organic Keywords**, click on the **Positions** filter, and enter "2-15".

These are the low-hanging fruit keywords you should attack right away. Then, click on the **Positions** dropdown and go to the custom range.

To take it a step further:

- Filter this set of keywords based on KD (Keyword Difficulty).

- Start with a max KD of 0 to find the lowest competition opportunities.

- Keep in mind: You'll also need to prioritize keywords based on intent and relevance.

The next type of keywords is from positions 16-50, which I label "existing." They're also good targets but should be second on the priority list after low-hanging fruits.

And the final category of keywords is from positions 51-100, which I call "clustering opportunities." If a page isn't ranking in the top fifty, then there's a good chance the ranking page isn't relevant enough.

For example, look at this keyword that Gotch SEO is ranking one hundredth for: "marketing companies Houston" with the "Houston SEO companies" page.

marketing companies houston	3	350	12	9.28	0	100	New	https://www.gotchseo.com/houston-seo-companies/ ▾

This page isn't relevant enough to rank for this long-tail keyword phrase. As a result, "Marketing companies Houston" is a clustering opportunity because you can create a dedicated page for this particular keyword phrase and rank much better. Plus, it will build more topical authority for the primary keyword: "Houston SEO companies."

Remember, Google's number-one goal is to deliver the most relevant results possible. With that said, these clustering opportunities are a terrific way to capture more organic search traffic and build more topical relevance, improving the performance of all pages in that cluster. Take advantage of it.

2. Steal ideas from your competitors

The purpose of an SEO content gap analysis is to find out what keywords our competitors are ranking for, but we are not. We can then create dedicated pages for the keywords to narrow the gap (and drive more organic search traffic).

Enter the domain into the Ahrefs Site Explorer and go to **Competing Domains** and sort by **Keywords unique to competitor** so the largest amount is at the top. Ignore big authority websites like Huffington Post or Forbes. Instead, focus on websites in the specific vertical.

Open **Content Gap** in another tab:

Enter three competitor domains into the **Content Gap**:

Pick domains that primarily focus on the topic/niche. Once again, don't pick authority websites like Forbes or Huffington Post because the results will be too broad.

Set the following filters: KD – "To 30" and "Volume – "From 100."

Now you'll see what keywords your competitors are ranking for, but your target website is not.

Qualify Your Keywords

Now that you've got a strong keyword list, it's time to qualify these opportunities.

The first filtering mechanism is to use Keyword Difficulty. No matter the strength of your website, I recommend looking at keywords with a KD of less than 30.

Then set a filter to only show keywords with a search volume greater than 100. And now, filter your keywords to only show those ranking in positions 2-15.

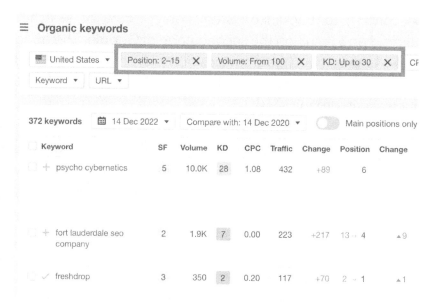

These are your low-hanging fruits. You should always start with these keywords because you are only a few tweaks away from capturing much more traffic.

In fact, according to a Backlinko study, the number-one spot gets roughly 27% organic CTR (Backlinko, 2022). That means for every one hundred searches, the number-one result will get twenty-seven visitors.

But here's where it gets even crazier: At number two, you'll get 15% CTR. That's a 44% decrease in organic traffic just by being one position lower.

To top it off, let's say you're ranking eleventh, putting you on page two.

According to Backlinko's study, only 0.63% of searches clicked on a result on the second page of Google. The good news is that if you go from position eleven on the second page to position ten, your CTR rises to 2.4%. That's a 280% increase in organic CTR.

The point is that most websites are already sitting on a potential goldmine of new traffic, leads, and sales if they bump up existing pages. Yet many people mistakenly believe that ranking success can only be achieved by publishing brand new content.

But now you know better. You need to focus on the low-hanging fruits and push those up first.

Let's get back to qualifying your keywords.

Now you should have a nice list of keywords with low keyword difficulty and decent search volume, ranking in solid positions.

The next question is, which keywords should you focus on within this group? The key to making that decision is completely based on search intent. In short, prioritize keywords with transactional intent toward the bottom of the funnel.

The best way to understand this is to review the five main categories of search intent which are Informational, Commercial / Investigative, Comparison, Transactional, and Navigational. Every strong SEO campaign will target keywords at each sales funnel stage.

Informational: Searcher is looking for broad information (e.g. garden gnome, nfl scores, SEO, etc) or wants the answer to a specific question e.g. "why...", "how to/many...", "what is...", "where is..." etc. Informational intent makes up the vast majority of searches.

Commercial / Investigative and Comparison: Searcher is investigating a specific product or service but hasn't necessarily made up their mind e.g. "best keyword research tool", "ahrefs vs semrush", "Ahrefs review" etc. These are often reviews and comparison-type searches. Can also include local searches e.g. "best accountant in St Louis", "top plumbers near me", etc.

Navigational: Searcher is looking for a specific website or page e.g. "LinkedIn login", "Amazon", "Gotch SEO" etc. These are commonly branded keywords and the searcher knows where they want to go but isn't sure of the URL or it's easier to just Google it than type the entire URL.

Transactional: Searcher is ready to buy or sign up e.g. "buy hd webcam", "Logitech webcam coupon", "sign up to Netflix", "order new iphone", "cheap laptop prices near me" etc.

So let's say you're building a keyword strategy for the Hoth SEO agency. At the top of the funnel, the Hoth would want to target keywords with informational intent like "how to write SEO content" or "how to build backlinks."

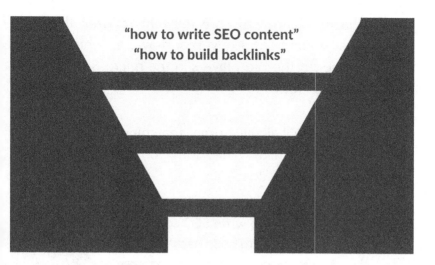

These keywords are broad and will drive the most traffic.

The next phase of the searcher journey is to target keywords with commercial or investigative intent like "buy backlinks" or "blog content writing services."

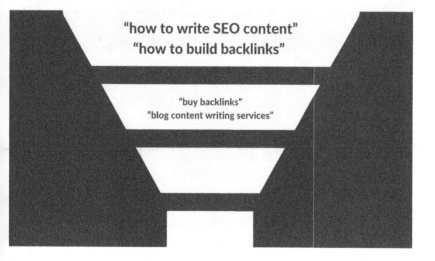

Notice that this is much more relevant to what the Hoth offers. The searcher is likely brand-aware, which means they know about the big players in the micro-SEO services market like the Hoth.

That means they'll likely begin searching keywords with navigational intent like "The Hoth" or comparison intent like "The Hoth vs Fat Joe."

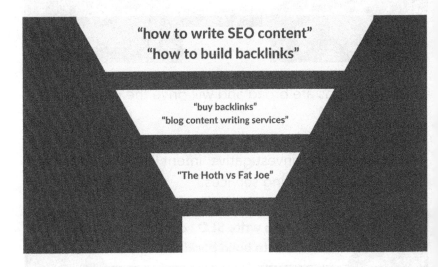

As you can tell, the searcher is getting very close to making a decision by weighing their options.

And now we've arrived at keywords with transactional intent, which in this case would be "the Hoth discount code" or "the Hoth pricing."

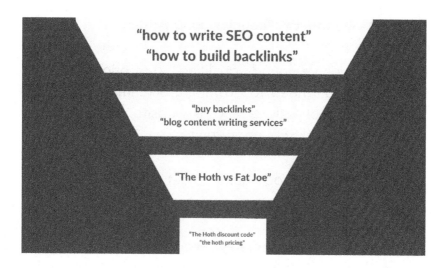

The conversion rate for keywords like this will be sky-high. So, you should always start at the bottom of the sales funnel and work your way up. Then, prioritize keywords with transactional intent and build your strategy to support those bottom-of-the-funnel keywords.

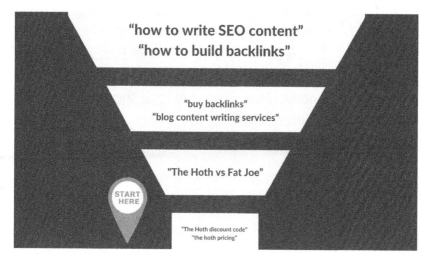

Step #2 - Conduct A Technical SEO Audit

Now that you've found, qualified, and prioritized your keywords, you'll need to download Screaming Frog SEO Spider. This tool will crawl your website and find every possible technical SEO opportunity.

Review Screaming Frog's guide to get started: https://www.screamingfrog.co.uk/seo-spider/user-guide/

Once the crawl is complete, I recommend exporting the report and adding it to a Google Sheet.

I could dedicate hours to this audit process, but here are three SEO opportunities to look out for:

Poor SEO Performance

Any indexable page that has no traffic (view Google Analytics), no impressions/clicks (view Google Search Console), and no backlinks (view Ahrefs) should be marked as "Poor SEO Performance."

Address	GA Sessions	Clicks	Impressions	Ahrefs Backlinks - Exact
https://legendarchery.com/blogs/archery-bowhunting-blog?page=17				0
https://legendarchery.com/blogs/archery-bowhunting-blog?page=18				0
https://legendarchery.com/blogs/archery-bowhunting-blog?page=19				0
https://legendarchery.com/blogs/archery-bowhunting-blog?page=20				0
https://legendarchery.com/blogs/archery-bowhunting-blog?page=21				0

You have a few options for handling poor-performing pages:

1. Upgrade & Optimize

You should upgrade and optimize when the page is important, but it wasn't developed properly. Sometimes you'll need to rebuild the asset from scratch. In many instances, you'll likely be using one of the other options below.

2. Delete & 404

A solid option for outdated, thin, or low-quality content that doesn't have any positive SEO KPIs. 404 errors aren't bad. In fact, a 404 error instructs Google's crawlers that a page no longer exists on the site. As a result, Google will pull it from the index, which is exactly what you want. Doing so will improve your crawl budget and eliminate index bloat.

3. Consolidate and 301 Redirect

Consolidation is a solid option if you want to retain content and use it on a different page. Sometimes it's wise to take many thin, poor-performing assets, turn them into one larger asset, and 301 redirect the old pages to the newly consolidated page.

4. Redirect

This option is only viable if the page has existing backlinks. Based on the filters above, no pages will qualify. However, if you loosen the filters and show pages with backlinks, but no other KPIs, then it is a solid option. The key is to 301 redirect to a relevant page on the website to retain the link authority.

5. Noindex, Follow

Using the "noindex, follow" tag is best for archive pages. In short, it instructs Google to remove the page from the index but continue to crawl it.

Handle these poor-performing pages at the onset of your SEO campaign, and you'll likely see some big improvements. The truth is that most pages are loaded with garbage and need pruning.

Internal Linking

Internal links help search engines crawl and index pages from your website. They also help distribute "PageRank" (or backlink authority) throughout your site.

Find Pages with Poor Crawl Depth

Crawl depth is how many clicks it takes to crawl a page on

your website. It's a critical part of optimization because it will determine how well Google crawls and indexes your site. The deeper pages are, the harder they are to crawl.

To find these pages, do the following:

1. Open up the Screaming Frog crawl export and make sure you're only looking at **Indexable** content. See the **Indexability** column.

2. Go to the **Crawl Depth** column > **Filter by Condition** > Greater than **3**:

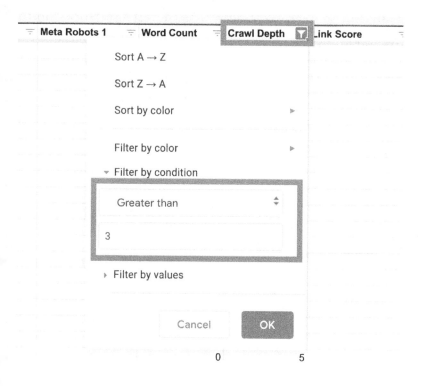

These are all the pages that are too many clicks deep into the site architecture.

How to Fix Crawl Depth

Now that you know how many internal links the target page has, it's time to decide the best path for pushing the page further up into the architecture. There are only a few methods you can use.

1. Build more internal links

The simplest solution is to find relevant pages on your website and add an internal link to the page with poor crawl depth. In the example below, I searched "YouTube" in the **Title** column.

This uncovered a common trend for "YouTube"-related pages. Almost all of them are buried deep in the architecture. That means it makes sense to interlink these posts because they're relevant.

Title 1	Crawl Depth	Link Score
How to Upload a Private Video on YouTube (2021)	5	
How to Share a Private Video on YouTube (2021)	5	
How to See YouTube Tags (2021)	4	
Miles Beckler Has Over 152,000 YouTube Subscribers (Here's How He Did It)	4	
SEO Audit #1 - YouTube.com	4	
10 Free Black Subscribe Buttons for YouTube	4	
10 Free Green Subscribe Buttons for YouTube	4	
10 Free Pink Subscribe Buttons for YouTube	4	
Do You Even Need a Youtube End Screen Template? 2021 Study	4	
How to Make Multiple Youtube Channels With One Email (2021)	4	
10 Free Blue Subscribe Buttons for YouTube	4	
How to Add Subscribe Button on YouTube Video (2021)	4	

It also makes sense to move on to the next technique:

2. Create A Hub Page

A "hub" page is a central location for linking to other relevant pages on a site. It's a powerful method because it builds topical relevance, increases internal link coverage, and eliminates crawl depth. Here's an example:

Start Learning Now With These SEO Resources

You can start learning SEO right now by diving into these resources.

General SEO

Best SEO Companies – We've analyzed hundreds of SEO companies throughout the United States to find out which ones are the best. Our rankings are 100% unbiased. Meaning, companies can't pay to be included on the list.

SEO Strategy – Every successful SEO campaign starts with a well-designed strategy. This guide will show you a simple 4-step strategy that has worked across nearly every vertical.

SEO Audit – The best way to start an SEO campaign is with a detailed audit. Properly performing an SEO audit will help you identify what to focus on. This is critical because not all SEO actions are created equally.

This page is designed to give coverage to "SEO"-related pages on our site.

So, by simply creating a similar "YouTube SEO" hub page, we can eliminate almost all crawl depth issues.

3. Leverage the Site-Wide Navigation

The easiest way to get more internal link coverage and to eliminate crawl depth is to leverage site-wide menus. This is particularly important for large websites like e-commerce stores with thousands of products.

Look at how Pottery Barn leverages their site-wide navigation and faceted navigation:

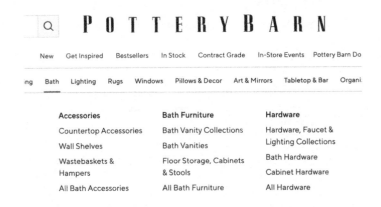

Find Pages with Poor Internal Link Coverage

Go to the **Unique Inlinks** column in Screaming Frog > **Filter by Condition** > Less than **5**.

We label any page with less than five internal links as "Not Enough Internal Link Coverage." All you need to do is A) look for relevant opportunities on the site to add internal links B) add the internal links and C) document your actions.

Find Authoritative Pages

"Authoritative" pages aren't an issue, but an opportunity. These pages are the best targets for building more internal links.

Go to the **Ahrefs RefDomains - Exact** column within Screaming Frog > **Filter by Condition** > Greater than or equal to **1**.

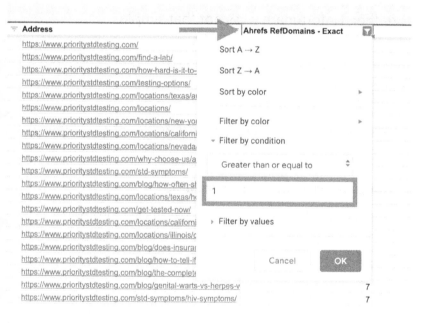

Prioritize pages with existing authority (backlinks) when building more internal links.

So those are a few technical SEO actions you can tackle right away. There are many more, but this will give you a solid start.

Step #3 - Optimize Existing SEO Content

After you've conducted a technical SEO audit outlined in the previous step, it's time to optimize some content. But first, a warning:

Some people think on-page SEO is just throwing your keywords on the page. That's like saying to prepare a great meal, all you need to do is throw a bunch of ingredients together. Unfortunately, it's not that simple.

And just like great cooking, there's an art and science to doing proper on-page SEO.

Here's a simplified version of what we do at our agency:

Is the page crawlable & indexable?

1. Install the Detailed SEO Extension on Chrome

2. Open the target page and click the extension:

3. Look under the **URL** section. It should say **Indexable**. Next, look under the **Robots Tag** section. It should say **Missing** or **follow, index**:

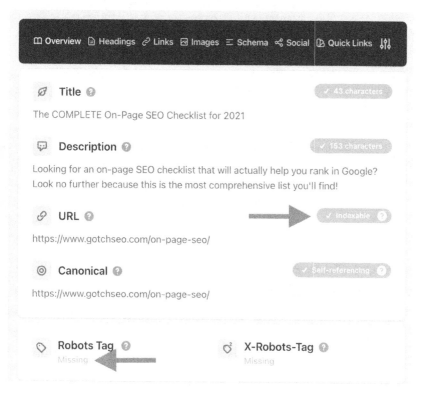

Does the page satisfy search intent?

The easiest way to answer this question is to examine the first page of results for the target keyword. First, go to Google, enter the target keyword, and ask what types of pages are ranking.

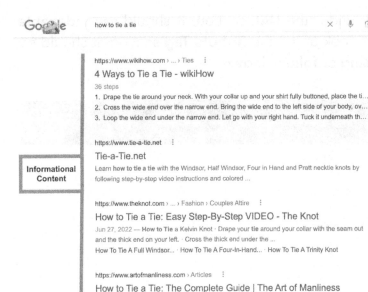

If most ranking pages are informational, then you should create an informational asset. On the other hand, you might create a transactional page (in most cases) if you see many transactional pages. Refer back to the "Qualify Your Keywords" section in Step 1 of this chapter if you need a quick refresher on search intent.

The idea is to simply model the competitors on the first page of Google regarding intent. Just remember that you're modeling the intent, not copying the content.

Does the page take a unique angle relative to the competitors?

You can satisfy intent while creating a unique content angle. For example, we wanted to target the keyword: "keyword research service." So, we analyzed the first results page and saw that all of them were transactional lead generation pages. But we knew this keyword had investigative intent.

So instead of creating a lead generation page, we took a unique angle and created a case study. In short, we purchased all the top keyword research services to see which are best. Then we created a list post detailing our experience and ranking the services. This unique angle quickly outperformed most competitors, and now the page ranks first.

Moral of the story? Invest time into finding unique angles while continuing to satisfy the intent.

Is the keyword placed in the right locations?

The primary keyword should be placed in the following locations at a bare minimum:

1. URL

2. Title Tag

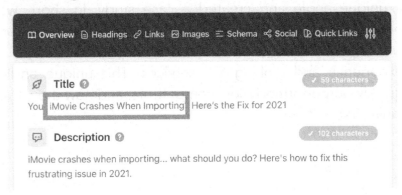

3. Meta Description

4. H1 Tag (usually the first visible heading on a page)

Your iMovie Crashes When Importing? Here's the Fix

April 11, 2021 by Nathan Gotch

5. First Sentence

If you're annoyed because your iMovie keeps crashing when importing, you're not alone! This is a common problem that many iMovie users face. It is so common, that by now you are probably wondering why it hasn't been solved. Video editing using iMovie can be a nightmare because of this.

6. First H2 Tag (often used for secondary headings)

You can use a variation here.

solutions that will surely help you.

Why is Your iMovie Crashing When Importing?

I'm an Apple MacBook Pro user at heart, and although I love their products, I get frustrated every time I try to import a video to iMovie. More often than not, I will get an

7. Last Sentence

You can use a variation here.

Conclusion

Don't despair if you feel frustrated. More likely than not, a solution always exists and has been shared by someone. I hope you found this article useful and most importantly, I hope you were able to solve you iMovie issues when importing files so that you can continue with your video editing.

These keyword placements are non-negotiable even if your favorite SEO tool tells you otherwise. Think of these as base-level optimization, and tools like Rankability supplement these efforts.

Is the page optimized for E-E-A-T / YMYL?

+ **EEAT** = Experience, Expertise, Authoritativeness, and Trustworthiness

+ **YMYL** = Your Money, Your Life

Google closely monitors industries like health, law, and finance because they could affect "Your Money" or "Your Life." That's why you must optimize all informational content for EEAT.

Every informational piece of content should have a qualified author or subject matter expert who reviews the content.

But, again, that needs to be evident on the page.

Here are some examples:

1. Page has an obvious author and fact-checker

**Vaccinated or Not, COVID-19 Testing
Is Still Important: Here's Why**

2. Citing and linking out to trusted sources of information

The Centers for Disease Control and Prevention (CDC) recently announced the first set of public health recommendations for fully vaccinated people. Bu safety during the pandemic, experts say there are still several

Trusted Source

**Centers for Disease Control
and Prevention (CDC)**

Governmental authority

Go to source

**How long do I have to wait u
protected by the vaccine?**

First, before you even consider a get-together with a friend, yo
are fully vaccinated and have waited the appropriate length of
immunity.

3. Dedicated section explaining editorial guidelines

✕

Healthline News Fact-Checking Standards

The Healthline News team is committed to delivering content that adheres to the highest editorial standards for accuracy, sourcing, and objective analysis. Every news article is thoroughly fact-checked by members of our Integrity Network. Furthermore, we have a zero-tolerance policy regarding any level of plagiarism or malicious intent from our writers and contributors.

All Healthline News articles adhere to the following standards:

1. All referenced studies and research papers must be from reputable and relevant peer-reviewed journals or academic associations.

2. All studies, quotes, and statistics used in a news article must link to or reference the original source. The article must also clearly indicate why any statistics presented are relevant.

3. All content related to new treatments, drugs, procedures, and so on must clearly describe availability, pricing, side effects, treatment target (e.g., HER2+), known interactions, and off-label use, if appropriate.

4. All news articles must include original commentary from at least two qualified sources with appropriate credentials and links to relevant associations or published works.

5. Any potential conflicts of interest related to a study or source must be clearly indicated to the reader.

6. All news articles must include appropriate background information and

4. Reemphasizing editorial guidelines

Healthline is raising the bar

At Healthline, we pride ourselves on the quality, research, and transparency we put into every article.

READ OUR QUALITY GUARANTEE

 All articles are thoroughly researched and reference high-quality studies and information to support the subject matter.

 Over 20,000 articles have been medically reviewed by doctors, nurses, and subject matter specialists.

 Our experts continually monitor the health and wellness space. As medical standards change or we get reader feedback, we update the information in our articles.

5. Uses citations for all information

— 10 sources

          FEEDBACK:

Healthline has strict sourcing guidelines and relies on peer-reviewed studies, academic research institutions, and medical associations. We avoid using tertiary references. You can learn more about how we ensure our content is accurate and current by reading our editorial policy.

* Barkataki S. (2021). Personal interview.

* Burke A, et al. (2017). Prevalence and patterns of use of mantra, mindfulness and spiritual meditation among adults in the United States.
ncbi.nlm.nih.gov/pmc/articles/PMC5472955/

* Chen KW, et al. (2012). Meditative therapies for reducing anxiety: A systematic review and meta-analysis of randomized controlled trials.
ncbi.nlm.nih.gov/pmc/articles/PMC3718554/

* Deekshitulu B. (2017). Stress management for mantra techniques.
medcraveonline.com/MOJYPT/stress-management-for-mantra-techniques.html

If the target keyword is informational, this is the standard. Remember, these standards should apply in every vertical (not just YMYL). It's the basis of creating trustworthy content in Google's eyes.

The only exception to "expertise" is "experience." Let's say you're doing reviews on different types of coffee. You don't need to be a barista to create these reviews. All you need is first-hand experience trying these coffees.

Is the page optimized for NLP?

Optimizing for NLP (Natural Language Processing) is not a requirement to rank, but it makes a big difference. You'll need to use an on-page SEO tool like Rankability to streamline this process.

First, open Rankability, go to the **Content Optimizer >
New Optimizer**, and enter your target keyword.

Then open the report and in the **Optimizer** Tab, make sure
it's sorted by **Importance**:

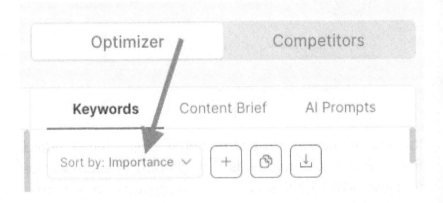

Begin adding these keyword variations through the copy
naturally. Like Rankability recommends, "Review the list of
important NLP keywords and add them to your content if it
makes sense."

Step #4 - Create New SEO Content

My philosophy for new SEO content is simple: create pages
that are different and better than what's currently ranking
for the target keyword.

Develop Your SEO Content Strategy

Go through each of these questions to develop a winning SEO content strategy:

1. What are the lagging goals for this content?

Your SEO content must have explicit goals. Sometimes people target keywords and have no real idea why they're doing it in the first place.

Some specific lagging SEO goals are:

* Increase organic search traffic
* Increase e-commerce revenue
* Increase lead volume

Whatever the case may be, always write out what your goals are for your SEO content.

2. Are we already targeting this keyword phrase?

Many websites make the mistake of targeting the same keyword on multiple pages (aka keyword cannibalization). As a result, you may confuse Google and force their algorithms to decide which page is best for the keyword. Not good. So go to your CMS and search the keyword to see if you're already targeting it.

3. What's the search intent?

You can use Semrush to identify the intent, but I still do this manually. Once again, refer back to the "Qualify Your Keywords" section in Step 1 of this chapter to get a more in-depth explanation of search intent. But here are some short guidelines:

- Top of the Funnel - Informational ("What is SEO?")
- Middle of Funnel - Commercial / Investigative ("Best SEO tools")
- Middle of Funnel - Comparison ("Moz vs Ahrefs")
- Bottom of Funnel - Transactional ("Moz free trial")

It's critical to identify the intent because it will dictate what type of content you'll create. For example, if the keyword is informational, you'll likely end up creating a blog post. If the keyword is transactional, you might create a product page with an offer.

4. What is the ideal word count?

Go into Rankability, enter your target keyword in the **Content Optimizer**, and get the typical word count for the top ranking pages.

Keep in mind Rankability's typical word count is a target but not a law. You have to use your best judgment. Sometimes keywords don't need as many words as the competition is showing.

For example, in the case of "iMovie crashing when importing," competitors had long pieces of content. And that's because they were writing about "iMovie crashing" in general, which is a much broader topic. But since I was only targeting the specific problem of "importing," it didn't require the exact word count.

Therefore, I ignored Rankability's word count suggestion in this scenario. That said, it's still helpful in getting a general idea of what direction to go.

5. Will this content need a subject matter expert?

I'm extreme and believe you should always try to find a subject matter expert to write or at least "review" your SEO content if possible. This rule mainly applies to informational content, but you should try to have your content bylined (using the writer's name) by a credible individual in the vertical. However, if you're creating a transactional or bottom-of-the-funnel page, it likely won't be necessary.

6. How many backlinks will we need?

Go to Ahrefs' **Keyword Explorer**, enter the target keyword, and look under the **KD** section to see how many backlinks you'll need:

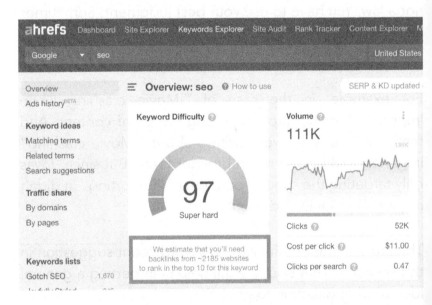

7. What's our unique angle for differentiation?

You need to brainstorm how your page will differ from the competitors for this keyword. The last thing you want to do is create another "me too" type of content. There's something to be said for modeling successful pages, but if you want long-term SEO results, you need to create unique content.

8. What types of graphics will we need?

You should always use custom graphics for your content whenever possible. *Everything* should be unique in your content. That applies to copywriting but also to images and videos. Don't worry, you don't have to be a graphic designer. One of the quickest ways to create unique graphics is to use Canva. You can take any picture, throw it on a background that uses your brand's color scheme, and then it becomes unique. Done.

9. Will this content require a photographer?

This question is for competitive keywords or keywords that require product images. If you're trying to rank product or category pages, your product images should be one hundred percent unique. And that typically means you'll need a photographer who can take professional product shots .

10. Will this content require a custom design?

A custom design can be a great way to differentiate your content. However, I only recommend using this method when it's super competitive and you're struggling to stand out in a crowded marketplace.

11. Will this content require custom filters or tools?

Depending on the keyword, you may need to create a tool or filter to satisfy the intent. For example, if I wanted to rank for "301 redirect checker," I would need to create a tool to satisfy the intent. Or, if I wanted to stand out for "Best SEO Companies," it would make sense to create a filtering system so the searcher could look for a company based on specific criteria.

12. What are five potential headlines for this content?

This is a critical step in the process that most people skip. Your headline is essential to your content because 80% of people don't read past the headline. So I always recommend brainstorming at least five different headline options. Then you should crosscheck the headline quality using a tool you can find online by Googling "free AM Institute Headline tool."

13. What are some related keywords?

Identifying keywords related to the primary topic is essential because you'll want to add these variations to your content to capture more organic search traffic.

Open Ahrefs' **Keyword Explorer** tool and enter the keyword. Then look through **Phrase match, Having same terms, Also rank for, Search suggestions, Newly discovered, and Questions:**

14. What are some topically relevant keywords that support (but don't compete with) the main topic?

After you add the relevant keywords with the same intent, it's important to identify keywords with different intent that supports the primary topic. That's because once you finish targeting your primary keyword, you should create new assets to support it. As a result, you'll build powerful relevance and topical authority on your website.

15. What is our call to action (CTA)?

Every single page on your website should have a call to action. Sometimes the CTA is "Please share this content," while other times it's a CTA for some middle-of-the-funnel asset like a lead magnet. The point is you must try to get the searcher to take the next stage in the relationship-building process. Try to push them further down the funnel.

16. What budget do we need?

Based on everything you've listed here, you can estimate your total budget to rank for this particular keyword.

One thing we like to do is use Fat Joe's pricing to estimate our budget. For example, let's say Fat Joe charges $219 for a two-thousand-word article. And it also charges between $61 - $493 for DA (Domain Authority from Moz) 10 to DA 50 backlinks. You can use the word count target and the backlink gap to get a solid estimated budget for this keyword. It's not a perfect science, but it can get you in the ballpark of what you'll need.

Create SEO Content Brief Template (for Writer)

At this point, you should already have an intense SEO content strategy brief. That doc is for internal use only and will help you develop a clear understanding of the keyword target. The "SEO Content Brief (for Writer)" is designed to help the writer create incredible content around the keyword. The more guidance you give them upfront, the less work you'll have to do in the revision process.

In short, you will take some of your findings from the SEO content strategy and move them onto this doc for the writer. Here's how to do it:

Part 1 - SEO

SEO Content Brief for Writer

<ENTER KEYWORD>: <# OF SEARCHES> /mo

	SEO
Title	
Meta Description	
Domain	
URL	
Word Count Target	
Primary Keyword	
Exact Keyword Mentions	
Secondary Keywords	
Phrases to Include	

In the first box labeled "SEO", enter:

Title - The exact title for the content. It needs to include the primary keyword.

Meta Description - The exact meta description you would like to use. It needs to include the primary keyword.

Target Domain - The domain where the content will be published.

URL - The future URL or current URL (if upgrading).

Word Count Target - Available in your SEO content strategy (giving a range is best).

Primary Keyword - The exact keyword you want to rank for.

Exact Keyword Mentions - Use a range here based on Rankability's recommendation.

Secondary Keywords - Keywords that have the same intent as the primary keyword.

Phrases to Include - Include 10-25 phrases (which you get from Rankability's Content Optimizer).

These phrases should not include primary or secondary

keywords. They are simply phrases that are closely related to the primary keyword. They're also useful because they can help the writer know what direction to go in.

Part 2 - Writing Guidelines

WRITING GUIDELINES	
Goal of Content	
Angle	
Audience	
Formality	
Tone	{Neutral | Confident | Joyful | Optimistic | Friendly | Urgent | Analytical | Respectful}
Domain	
Intent	{To Educate | To Inspire | To Entertain | To Persuade}
CTA	
Models	
Formatting	Use short paragraphs (1-3 sentences), headings, subheadings, bullet points, and numbered lists.
Images	Use screenshots, charts, diagrams, etc. (Cite where you found the

Goal of the Content - Keep it simple here, such as "Rank #1 for {Keyword}," or "Get more organic search traffic and leads."

Angle - Essential for guiding the writer in the right direction.

Audience - What level of expertise or focus will the reader need to understand the content? The answer will determine whether or not you need a subject matter expert (SME for short) to create the content.

For example, if you're creating content about "funny cat pictures," your audience would fall under "General," and you likely wouldn't need an SME. However, if you are creating content about "Python for SEO," you should work with a seasoned developer to create it since the topic falls under the "expert" level audience. Use your best judgment and common sense here.

Formality - If it's B2B, you'll want a more neutral or formal tone. If it's B2C, you can get more informal.

Tone - Pick one or two of the options: {Neutral | Confident | Joyful | Optimistic | Friendly | Urgent | Analytical | Respectful}

Domain - This applies to the website's vertical. In short, it's how free the writer can get with traditional writing conventions. Here are the options:

- **Academic:** Strictly applies all rules and formal writing conventions.

- **Business:** Applies almost all rules but allows some informal expressions.

- **General:** Applies most rules and conventions with medium strictness.

- **Casual:** Applies most rules but allows stylistic flexibility.

- **Creative:** Allows some intentional bending of rules and conventions.

Intent - If it's an informational keyword, it will likely fall under "Educate." If it's an investigative or transactional keyword, it will likely fall under "Persuade." Here are some examples: {To Educate | To Inspire | To Entertain | To Persuade}.

CTA - Enter a call to action that's appropriate for the keyword's intent. For example, if it's informational, you could write, "If you found this tutorial helpful, please share it!" You could also send the user another helpful piece of top-of-the-funnel content. Or you could push them to a middle-of-the-funnel piece of content like a lead magnet that requires an email.

Models - Enter one to three URLs for the writer to model. These content models should not necessarily be for the primary keyword you're targeting because this may lead to too many similarities between your content and the models . Instead, you can pick examples from URLs targeting different keywords that you want your writer to emulate in terms of style and structure.

Formatting - I've given a default recommendation for "Formatting" because this is best for Internet readability.

Feel free to modify as you please - "Use short paragraphs (1-3 sentences), headings, subheadings, bullet points, and numbered lists."

Images - This may not always apply to the writer, but if it's an instructional piece of content, it may make sense to add screenshots. Once again, you'll need to modify this section based on the keyword.

Part 3 - Links

LINKS		
Type	Target URL	Anchor Text

The goal of this section is to add any internal or external links you believe are important for this content.

Part 4 - Outline

OUTLINE

Don't go crazy here. Keep it broad and let the writer work their magic. Your job isn't to micromanage them. The outline should give them enough information to use their expertise to create something extraordinary. So I typically only include some basic instructions and let the writer take it from there.

Now , if you've done all the previous steps well, you'll likely see significant rankings and organic traffic gains. However, there's one last step you'll need to take.

Step #5 - Acquire Backlinks

The first question is, what are backlinks?

Backlinks are created when one website links to another website. Google (and other search engines) consider backlinks to be "votes" for a page. In fact, Google's original PageRank algorithm used backlinks to signal content quality. And since then, many studies have found a direct correlation between backlinks and organic search engine rankings.

Here's an example of a backlink:

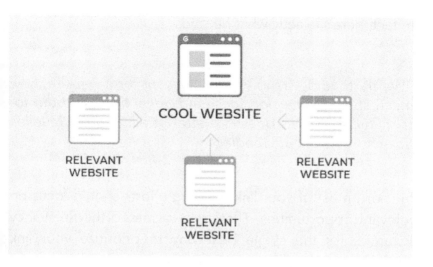

Over time, the types of backlinks you acquire have become even more important. For example, back in the day, you could get any type of backlink and it would boost your rankings. Those days are long gone.

7 Characteristics of Quality Backlinks

High-quality backlinks have seven characteristics: relevance, traffic, authority, link profile quality, editorial standards, outbound link quality, and indexation.

1. Relevance

As Google's Search Advocate, John Mueller has stated that relevance is more important than how many backlinks a website has.

In fact, here's exactly what he said:

"We try to understand what is relevant for a website, how much should we weigh these individual links, and the total number of links doesn't matter at all." - John Mueller, Search Advocate at Google

In short, most of your link building efforts should focus on relevant opportunities. That's why I created the Relevancy Pyramid. It's the single best way to prioritize your link opportunities.

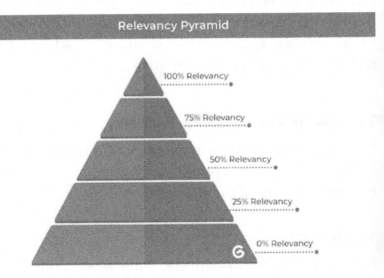

The model is simple. There will be fewer link building opportunities that are one hundred percent relevant to your website. You should focus on these first. For example, if you're trying to rank a website about coffee makers, you'd try to find high-quality link opportunities from reputable websites in the coffee niche. Then, once you've tapped those out, move down the pyramid to perhaps websites in the food and beverage niche where there will be more link prospects but slightly less relevant. And so on.

Now there are two exceptions to this link prioritization strategy:

- Getting legit links from super authority sites like the New York Times, Washington Post, or .edu or .gov sites is always okay.

- The Relevancy Pyramid changes if you're working in local SERPs.

For local SEO, I recommend focusing on geo-targeted opportunities first. Then, move on to topically relevant prospects on the national level.

This will create the most natural and relevant link profile.

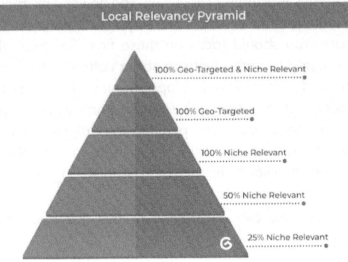

Local Relevancy Pyramid

- 100% Geo-Targeted & Niche Relevant
- 100% Geo-Targeted
- 100% Niche Relevant
- 50% Niche Relevant
- 25% Niche Relevant

Now, of course, it's not all about relevance. If that were the case, you could create hundreds of relevant websites yourself and link to your site. That doesn't work because it would miss all the other factors that make a backlink powerful.

2. Traffic

You need to get links to your site from relevant websites with organic traffic. Think about it: What does it say if Google sends organic search traffic to a site? Well, when you consider that 91% of all websites never receive a single visitor from Google, it means that Google thinks it's likely a trustworthy website.

Generally speaking, sites that are popular in organic search are valuable link-building opportunities.

You can use Ahrefs or Semrush to see if a website is getting organic search traffic (and to see the estimated "value" of that traffic):

Traffic *i*
12.3K 31.63%

Traffic Cost *i*

$56.7K 26.22%

3. Authority

If a website is getting organic traffic, it likely has authority. You can use Ahrefs' Domain Rating (DR) to prioritize link building prospects based on their site authority.

The higher the DR, the stronger their authority and backlink profile.

SEO Training & Consulting with Nathan Gotch

gotchseo.com ▾

Ahrefs Rank *i*	UR *i*	DR *i*	Backlinks *i*	Referring domains *i*
62,332	27	72	38.2K −40	3.07K
			Recent 68.9K	Recent 3.51K
			Historical 224K	Historical 6.53K

And the stronger a website is, the harder it will be to get the link. That makes those links even more valuable, so it's worth the effort.

4. Link Quality

Unfortunately, it is possible for shady individuals to sometimes manipulate third-party metrics like Ahrefs' DR or Moz's DA, so you need to manually analyze the backlink profile of all your opportunities. I like to run the website through Ahrefs and filter their links by **Dofollow**.

Latest Firefox Release Available today for iOS and Desktop - The Mozilla Blog 🔒 blog.mozilla.org/blog/2019/07/09/latest-firefox-release-available-today-for-ios-and-desktop/ ▾ EN WORDPRESS	95	41	187
US7680648.pdf docs.google.com/viewer?url=patentimages.storage.googleapis.com/pdfs/US7680648.pdf ▾ EN	95	20	51
Apache Spark on Amazon EMR - Amazon Web Services 🔒 aws.amazon.com/emr/features/spark/ ▾ EN	95	29	52

Do follow links are important because they can be crawled by search engines like Google and they pass on link equity (aka "link juice") to your site.

I then sort them so that the strongest links with the highest DR are at the top. In short, you want to see the site getting links from high-quality sources. Use the same criteria from above.

5. Editorial Standards

Why are diamonds valuable? Because they're in high demand and difficult to get! That's why you should focus on getting links from websites with high editorial standards.

In other words, sites that place a high value on content quality and have strict guidelines on who they will send links to.

Guidelines

The Editorial Guidelines are the BBC's values and standards. They apply to all our content, wherever and however it is received.

The harder it is to land a backlink, the more valuable it is. The opposite is true, as well: if a backlink is easy to acquire, it's usually less valuable.

6. Outbound Link Quality

Websites with strong editorial guidelines will likely only link out to quality resources. You want your link to "live" around other trustworthy outbound links.

Enter your domain into Ahrefs **Site Explorer** and go to **Linked domains** under **Outgoing links**:

Examine every prospective website and ask:

- How are they linking out?

- Are the outbound links relevant?

- Are the outbound links going to respected, trusted sites?

- Do the outbound links look natural (i.e. they could be naturally acquired without asking), or do they look like paid links?

7. Indexation

Nothing is more important than making sure you get links on indexed websites. If the site isn't indexed by Google, then your links will be worthless.

Go to Google and search "site:example.com" (replace "example.com" with the website you're considering getting a backlink from).

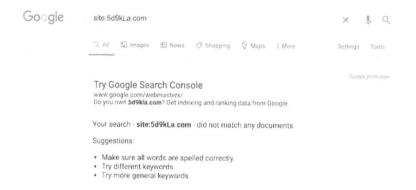

If no pages show up (i.e. you see "Your search did not match any documents."), avoid the website.

Now that you know what a quality backlink looks like, let's talk about what links you should *avoid like* the plague.

3 Types of Backlinks to Avoid

If you review the seven characteristics of quality backlinks above, you'll notice that the following types of backlinks don't qualify.

In other words, most websites aren't relevant, don't have traffic, have poor link quality, no editorial guidelines, and have horrific outbound links. Here's the first example:

1. Public Blog Networks

You've probably heard of Private Blog Networks (PBNs), but public blog networks differ. Both are risky because it's artificial link building. However, private blog networks are slightly less risky because they can be disguised better.

Public blog networks, on the other hand, are nothing more than link farms that are easily detectable. Look at this website that uses public blog network links:

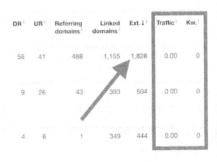

The red flag is having a ton of external links coupled with zero traffic.

Most public networks don't even bother to block third-party crawlers like Ahrefs. The truth is, if it takes me two seconds to see that you're using public network links, then what do you think Google can do?

Here's what an actual public blog network looks like:

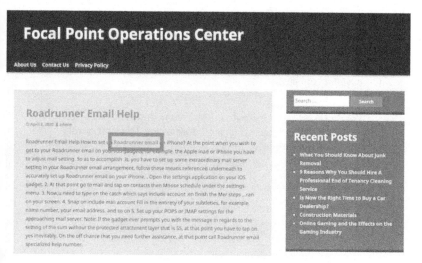

The tell-tale signs include having minimal pages in the navigation bar, using very basic or outdated themes, and content that isn't user-friendly (i.e. long paragraphs, no images, etc) and looks as though the entire purpose was to link to another site.

A good question to ask yourself is, *"Would anyone actually visit this site on purpose?"*

If the answer is no, stay away from these links if you want to avoid getting penalized.

2. Dofollow Blog Comments

You've probably seen these countless times but here's what they look like:

1,237 responses about "Can you really make money while you sleep?"

1. davidjackson said:
November 6th, 2018 at 5:54 am

Very interesting website it is. I saw many different posts here and all are very interesting and informative. This post is very unique and informative for all. Impressive information you share in this. Keep it up and keep sharing.
click here for gymnastic mats

2. Chris said:
November 7th, 2018 at 8:22 am

You are lucky enough to earn that amount while you're not doing anything. Well, this inspires everyone who wants to earn. Appreciation from Leland Towing.

3. Mumbai-Escorts said:
November 8th, 2018 at 7:11 am

Today i came across this article and i must say this is the best article that i read so far. Great Post!!.
I would like to read more on this topic as it was very interesting to read.

These links hit the "authority" quality criteria for links. However, they greatly miss the mark with everything else. Plus, you don't want your website in the same neighborhood as some of the outbound links you'll see.

3. Web 2.0s

The thought process for using web 2.0s is similar to dofollow blog comments. You're trying to leverage the existing site's authority like Wix:

🌐 https://johndoe123.wixsite.com/mysite/post/1

However, web 2.0s add another level because they attempt to create artificial relevance.

First and foremost experience and focus for the lawyer matters a lot with regards to how well they are able to handle situations and how vastly they have knowledge anti-white capable in representing all your interest to the best of your expectations as you would want. Their determination and drive of how they handle issues in particular will go a long way to determine whether or not you get to have this problem solved in totality. In addition to this you must also look at the client testimonials and reviews from previous cases that may be of similar nature so that you get to the best regard how well they have in the previous issues handled the matters. Accessibility and reliability plays a role which is integral with regard to location and how easily both parties can meet during the time period for which the case in question is being sorted out and above all to have a situation that is most likely comfortable with both parties. Another factor to look at is the cost that you will have to in car in terms of finances for your case to be hard and solution attained at the end of the day. Finally the above-mentioned considerations form part of the most important when it comes to seeking for the services of a personal injury lawyer. check out here new york injury lawyer.

View more here https://youtu.be/tlESkR/RKR8.

So, what's the problem? Well, they aren't editorial links, the content is low-quality, and you don't benefit much from the authority because it's on a subdomain. Plus, the only way web 2.0 backlinks can have any benefit is if they're indexed. And guess what?

They're notoriously hard to index.

How to Get Backlinks (Like an SEO Pro)

Here are seven link building techniques you can use to land high-quality backlinks.

1. Authority Transfer Technique

The Authority Transfer Technique isn't technically a "link building" tactic, but it's a powerful way to distribute link authority (PageRank) to your most important SEO-driven pages.

Step #1 – Identify what pages on your site have existing backlinks

Once again, the easiest way to find these pages is to use Ahrefs.

Open up Ahrefs → Site Explorer → Enter your domain → Start analysis

Then click on "Best by Links" under "Pages" → Sort by "Referring Domains":

#	Page	UR	Referring domains ↓	External links Dofollow
1	How to Build Backlinks in 2019 (NEW Guide) | Gotch SEO www.gotchseo.com/backlinks/ ▼ EN WORDPRESS	45	340	890
2	Gotch SEO www.gotchseo.com/ ▼ WORDPRESS	42	252	295
3	Anchor Text Guide for 2019 | Gotch SEO www.gotchseo.com/anchor-text/ ▼ EN WORDPRESS	41	226	650

Step #2 – Add internal links on those pages to relevant SEO-driven pages

All you need to do now is add internal links targeting pages that are A) topically relevant and B) you're trying to rank. I recommend using exact-match anchor text (the text you use for a link) with your internal links which is safe to do so as long as they aren't site-wide.

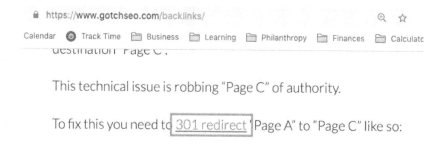

This technical issue is robbing "Page C" of authority.

To fix this you need to 301 redirect "Page A" to "Page C" like so:

I recommend using this technique every time you publish a new SEO-driven page. It's one of the best ways to give your page a boost out of the gate by leveraging existing authority. Your goal should be to push your pages up the SERPs as far as possible before acquiring links. The Authority Transfer Technique is one of the best ways to accomplish that goal quickly .

2. LIS Technique

What qualities make people want to link to your website? While there are many, there's one in particular that helps enormously and it's called "Length Implies Strength" or LIS.

Ever seen one of those super-long sales letters that seem to scroll for decades?

Well, that's not an accident. Long sales letters actually leverage something called Heuristics (Psychology Today, 2022). In short, we humans are lazy and hate thinking. So we use mental shortcuts to make decisions, solve problems, pass judgments, etc.

What does this have to do with link building?

According to a Backlinko study: "Long-form content gets an average of 77.2% more links than short articles (Backlinko, 2022)."

So if you want more backlinks? Create long-form, high-quality content. For example, if you examine what pages have attracted the most backlinks on GotchSEO.com, you'll notice they're all my best and longest pieces of content:

#	Page	UR	Referring domains ↓
1	How to Build Backlinks in 2019 (NEW Guide) | Gotch SEO 🔒 www.gotchseo.com/backlinks/ ▾ EN WORDPRESS	45	340
2	Gotch SEO 🔒 www.gotchseo.com/ ▾ WORDPRESS	42	252
3	Anchor Text Guide for 2019 | Gotch SEO 🔒 www.gotchseo.com/anchor-text/ ▾ EN WORDPRESS	41	226
4	Best SEO Blog 🔒 www.gotchseo.com/blog/ ▾ EN WORDPRESS	36	150
5	SEO Audit Checklist for 2019 [NOT for Beginners] | Gotch SEO 🔒 www.gotchseo.com/seo-audit/ ▾ WORDPRESS	36	143
6	301 moved permanently www.gotchseo.com/ ▾ ↳ 🔒 www.gotchseo.com/ ▾	36	122
7	Ahrefs: The Ultimate Guide 🔒 www.gotchseo.com/ahrefs/ ▾ EN WORDPRESS	34	108

The average word count for my top four most linked-to content assets is 7,223 words.

Pretty insane, right? Here's the main takeaway: If you want more links, write longer, in-depth content. Don't take this out of context, though! It needs to be well-thought-out and add massive amounts of UNIQUE value.

3. Predictive Links Technique

What if you could create pages on your site that attracted backlinks like clockwork? That's possible when you use the Predictive Links Technique. The best part? It's super simple. Here's what you do:

Step #1 – Examine your competitor's most linked-to pages

Open up Ahrefs → Site Explorer → Enter a competitor's domain → Click on **Best by Links**

#	Page	UR	Referring domains ↓	External links ⌐ Dofollow
1	How to Build Backlinks in 2019 (NEW Guide) | Gotch SEO 🔒 www.gotchseo.com/backlinks/ ▾ EN WORDPRESS	45	340	890
2	Gotch SEO 🔒 www.gotchseo.com/ ▾ WORDPRESS	42	252	295
3	Anchor Text Guide for 2019 | Gotch SEO 🔒 www.gotchseo.com/anchor-text/ ▾ EN WORDPRESS	41	226	650

You'll immediately see what topics have attracted the most backlinks in your niche.

You can also use this same technique for creating "predictively" viral content on social.

Just go to Buzzsumo.com → Content Discovery → Enter a topic

Then, you'll have access to proven ideas to attract social shares (and links).

You can also do the same thing with YouTube. Go to a popular channel in your niche → sort their videos by most popular:

And BOOM! You see the ideas that the niche is most interested in.

Step #2 – Create a page on the same topic, but make it ten times different and better

Whether you're using this method to attract links, get more social traction, or dominate YouTube, the principle is the same. You will create a content asset that's ten times different and better than your competitors.

Step #3 – Reach out to the people that linked to your competitor's content

I recommend testing the waters (a concept I teach in Gotch SEO Academy) before pitching your content when you use this strategy. Send a simple outreach email like this:

Hey [NAME],

My name is [YOUR NAME], and I'm the [YOUR POSITION] at [YOUR COMPANY]. I researched [TOPIC] and saw that you linked to [COMPETITOR'S URL] – which makes sense because it's awesome. I just published a new guide on [TOPIC]. It [VALUE PROPOSITION].

Would you be interested in seeing it (and maybe give some feedback)? Let me know, and I'll shoot the link over.

Thanks again!

[YOUR NAME]

If the prospect complies, then send them this:

Hey [NAME],

That's great! Here's a link:

Let me know what you think.

Also, if you think it adds value to your readers, would you mind linking to it? I can [INSERT SOME VALUE YOU CAN GIVE THEM]. Thanks again!

I recommend testing many different templates for the second email until you hit a sweet spot. Just make sure you're giving something valuable when asking for a link.

4. Relationship Accelerator Technique

The Relationship Accelerator Technique serves a dual purpose:

1. It can help you build relationships with key "linkerati" (people who are capable and willing to link to you).

2. It can help you score links with minimal effort.

There are a few different ways to go about this. You can host expert roundups, host interviews, or ask for expert contributions to your content. For example, I had Miles Beckler on my SEO podcast, and he linked to the page where it was hosted:

1. Publish transcriptions from your podcasts to your blog, like this: https://shontavia.com/transcript34/

2. Create a blog category for your podcast and publish every episode with show notes, like this: http://www.youtubecreatorshub.com/111-a-video-a-day-for-90-days-with-miles-beckler/

3. Create blog posts that are optimized to rank for your guest's name, like this: https://www.gotchseo.com/miles-beckler/

This technique works because there's a clear exchange of value. The experts get exposure, and you get to build a non-transactional relationship with them. You'll also be promoted because they will likely share or link to the content.

5. Oprah Technique

I created a cool name for this technique, but it's super simple. You're going to get interviewed and land links.

Go to Google → Enter "interview + niche" or "interview with + [YOUR COMPETITOR]"

Add all these prospects to your link-building database. Then, just reach out and pitch yourself for the interview.

Use a simple template like this:

Hey [NAME],

My name is [YOUR NAME] and I'm the [YOUR POSITION] at [YOUR COMPANY]. First, just wanted to thank you for all the amazing interviews you've been doing. I've listened to your interview with [INSERT ONE YOU LIKED] multiple times because it's so incredibly valuable. Quick question: are you accepting new interviewees at this time? If you are, I would love to chat because of [COOL RESULT].

Let me know. Thanks!

6. The Merger Technique

The Merger Technique is simple: Find websites with high-quality link profiles, acquire them, and 301 redirect them to your website.

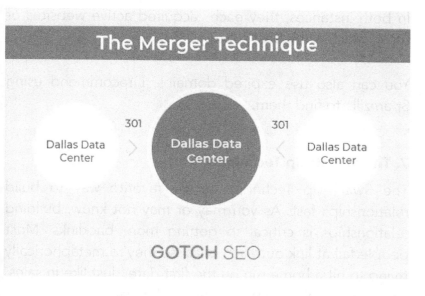

For example, Neil Patel acquired UberSuggest and merged it with NeilPatel.com. As a result, he gained an additional 17,500 backlinks from 5,610 referring domains:

And Backlinko (aka Brian Dean) did the same thing when he acquired PointblankSEO.com. Brian scored 24,500 additional backlinks from 2,000 referring domains:

In both instances, they each acquired active websites or tools, which is the best strategy.

You can also use expired domains. I recommend using Spamzilla to find them.

7. The Switch-Up Technique

The Switch-Up Technique is my favorite way to build relationships fast. As you may or may not know, building relationships is critical to getting more backlinks. Most people fail at link outreach because they're metaphorically trying to hit a home run on the first date. Just like in sales, you need to take baby steps along the way .

You have to build relationships with the websites (and people who are capable of linking to you) *before* you ask for something. There needs to be an exchange of value.

Value comes in many forms, including money, help, and content. Here's a perfect example of a former student of Gotch SEO Academy (our SEO training program) exchanging value with me – I had no choice but to link to this tool because it solved a real problem and added *real* value:

Brandyn Morelli
to me

Hey Nathan,

I noticed in your article The Only SEO Strategy You Need in 2018 | Gotch SEO that you reference
https://wordcounter.net/website-word-count for a word counter tool.

I've been using the same tool for a while, but it's been time intensive to manually enter in each URL so I've
created a new free tool that can copy/paste up to 10 URL's at a time to speed up the process.

It also gives you the average word count too so you can get an idea of the length a new article should have.
If you think it could be helpful you can access it here: https://brightlab.co/seo-word-counter (no opt-in or
anything).

Anyways thanks for the great content,

Brandyn

Offering money for links works well, but you can also acquire links without having to pay people. But that will only be possible through building real relationships. The first step to accomplishing that is to use the Switch-Up Technique.

Here's how you do it:

1. Go through your blog content and examine all your external links.

2. See if you're linking out to general websites like Wikipedia, CNN, or any authority website with many authors.

3. Go to Google and look for a replacement from a lower authority blog.

4. Change your link

5. Reach out to the lower authority blog writer.

Use a non-threatening template like this:

Hey [NAME],

My name is [YOUR NAME] and I'm the [POSITION] at [COM-PANY]. I was doing some research on [TOPIC] and discovered your guide about [TOPIC]. I really enjoyed it. I never realized that [SOMETHING YOU LEARNED FROM THEIR CONTENT]. Super cool. Anyway, I won't take up any more of your time. Just wanted to thank you for putting the article together and wanted to let you know that I linked to it from my article: [INSERT NAKED URL] – it's about [TOPIC].

Thanks again!

[YOUR NAME]

Conclusion + Next Steps

Congratulations – you made it to the end of this book! You're already ahead of 80% of people who never make it past the first chapter.

And you're probably feeling a bit overwhelmed right now because I know this was an intense read. But you've just concluded the total immersion training to building a successful SEO business from scratch. And you now have exactly what you need to get started today.

But here's the deal:

If you want to take it a step further and surround yourself with other six, seven, and even a few eight-figure SEO professionals, then I recommend applying for Gotch SEO Academy – my exclusive training and coaching program.

First, you'll get access to three SEO certification programs: SEO Specialist, SEO Expert, and SEO Mastery. These are the only programs you'll ever need to succeed with SEO. But that's not all.

You'll also get access to our weekly coaching sessions. These are held by me (Nathan Gotch) every Tuesday and Thursday. That means you can ask me any questions about growing your SEO business or any SEO campaigns you're working on.

And lastly, you'll get access to our private community, where you can get all the support from me and our hundreds of successful GSA members 24/7.

Go to gotchseo.com to apply today.

Once again, thank you so much for allowing me to be your SEO guide. I truly appreciate your trust, attention, and sincerely wish you the best of luck in your SEO and entrepreneurial journey.

P.S. I've also included a bonus section showing you thirty lessons I've learned running a seven-figure SEO agency for ten years. Enjoy.

Bonus: 30 Lessons from Running a Successful 7-Figure SEO Company for 10 Years

"Dear Red, If you're reading this, you've gotten out. And if you've come this far, maybe you're willing to come a little further..." - The Shawshank Redemption

Here's the big idea:

I wanted to share as many lessons as I can from the last decade of running a successful SEO agency so you don't have to make the same mistakes that I did.

The goal is to help you achieve success much faster than I did with fewer headaches.

Warning: I may get a little "self-help-y" because I'm speaking from real experience. If you're cool with that, let's dive in:

Marketing Lessons

1. Practice What You Preach

Believe it or not, some SEO companies don't even rank their own site on Google.

What's a better demonstration of competency: an SEO company that blasts businesses with cold calls? Or an SEO company that ranks well in the world's #1 search engine? It's a no-brainer.

I get 99% of my leads from the two biggest search engines (Google & YouTube). The best part about practicing what you preach is that it makes selling SEO a hundred times easier. All you have to say is, "Well, how did you find us?" – BOOM. The proof is in the pudding.

The idea of practicing what you preach applies to any service business. You should be able to prove that you know what the heck you're doing. Don't say you're an SEO "expert" if you've never ranked a keyword. Don't say you're a social media marketing "expert" when you only have fifty followers on Twitter. Don't say you're a PPC "expert" if you have never made an ROI on ad spend.

You get the point. Practice what you preach. Go out and get results on your own. It will not only build credibility but also skyrocket your close rate.

2. Testimonials & Referrals Won't Come Organically

Unfortunately, it doesn't matter how well you get results and how happy your SEO clients are. In most cases, they will not go out of their way to give you a testimonial or send you a referral. It is what it is.

Think about it: they are either A) busy running a business or B) acting as marketing directors for a company. So, they don't arrive at work and think: "You know what I should do today? I need to write a testimonial for our SEO company and spend my day finding referrals for them!"

That's why you need to "gently encourage" (i.e. ask) your clients to give you testimonials and referrals. . And sometimes asking isn't enough. To get your clients to act, you might even consider offering an incentive.

For example, we offer clients a free month of SEO service when they send us a referral that signs up as a client. . A free month of SEO service is valuable, considering they are saving at least $5,000+.

Sales Lessons

3. Be Responsive to Leads (Or Lose)

It's easy to sit back when you see an inbound lead. But every second you waste is a second the prospect gets less interested in you. It also gives your competition another second to call before you.

You thought you were the only company they contacted? Don't fool yourself. Businesses will reach out to at least three to five companies for a significant investment like SEO.

Being the first to respond is sometimes all it takes to win contracts. Clients have told me they picked my agency because we responded so quickly. Bottom line: The early bird gets the worm.

4. You Don't Have to Be a Stereotypical Used Car Salesman

Good news: If you're using inbound marketing to generate leads (and you should be); there is no reason to be pushy. You aren't making a cold call. The lead has gone out of their way to contact you.

So get on a call or online meeting with them, be calm, cool, and collected, and see if they're a good fit for your services. No slimy or high-pressure tactics required.

And you should always try to close on the call or, at the very least, make a solid offer. . Just understand that most businesses will need time to discuss and review proposals.

You can often close on the call if you are speaking with a smaller business. However, if you are speaking with a CMO or marketing director, it will likely take weeks for them to decide. Which is fine; the fortune is in the follow-up.

Mindset Lessons

5. You're Disposable (No Matter How Good You Are)

If you take anything out of this, please ensure this is it. No matter how good your service is, you or your agency are always disposable. And the client is always going to value their business over yours.

SEO will be one of their first cuts if they have financial issues or the market takes a downturn. It doesn't matter how buddy-buddy you are with the client. Remember this lesson if you're ever tempted to do anything less than your best on an SEO campaign. Treat every client like gold – that's how you win.

6. Be Selfish

I'm all about the client-first mantra, but ultimately why are we in business? Most of us are in business to achieve financial freedom and live better lives.

So, why do so many of us work ourselves to death over a single client?

I'm not implying that you should do shoddy work, but you need to stop acting like you are a commodity. Have boundaries.

Let's say a client pays you $500 monthly, and your rate is $100 an hour. Then you should only work five hours a month for that client. Do not let the client convince you otherwise.

Understand that you teach people how they treat you. So by accepting more work from a demanding client than what was originally agreed upon (aka "scope creep"), you're creating a monster.

If you work a single second longer on that client, it will take away from other clients. Not only that, but it will also take away precious time for you to work *on* your business instead of in it.

7. Be Cheap

When I first started my agency, it was just many virtual assistants (VAs) and me. I outsourced everything and paid stupid amounts of money for link placements. Unfortunately, some of these vendors scammed me, and many of the link placements sucked or got removed.

Besides setting a strict time budget like the previous lesson explained, you must also set a monetary budget for each client. For example, I typically allocate (and recommend) up to 30% of a client's monthly retainer for all expenses (i.e. outsourcing, content, link buying, etc) which leaves me with a healthy 70+% profit margin.

Keep in mind that some months that budget may vary a little depending on the needs of the client. And if you're just starting out, your profit margin may be lower in the beginning from working with lower client retainers – which is fine and to be expected.

But a good long-term goal is to aim for a 70% profit margin from your SEO business.

8. Never Get Complacent

You must focus on growing YOUR business every single day. Never think that your clients are going to work with you forever. Because they won't. Always work with the mindset that you could lose all your income tomorrow.

Will this happen? Not likely. But never get complacent with what you have. Always keep pushing and trying to grow.

Grow or die.

But this goes back to one of my original points: "Be Selfish." You have to keep trying to grow your business. No matter how many clients you have. No matter how much money you are already making.

Now, don't get me wrong. This is not about lacking gratitude or never having enough. In fact, it's quite the opposite.

If you are fortunate enough to have a successful SEO agency, it's your duty to focus on growth like you don't have a single client. It's a survival mechanism. Have the mindset that you could lose it all tomorrow. Take it from me, complacency will kill your business.

9. Stop Being A Commodity and Become an Asset

Give your client so much value that it would be painful for them to stop paying you. When you reach that stage, you become a true asset. You can demand prices you think are fair instead of the prospect telling you how much you should get paid. Always remember that price is nothing more than the perceived value. The more valuable you are to a company, the more they will pay.

10. Avoid Startups/Young Businesses

As a general rule of thumb, I recommend you avoid any "startup" company or very young business. Many of these businesses likely cannot afford your services.

But even if they can, they often think it's easier to hire someone to grow their business. Truth be told, they are creating an environment where they rely on other people to be successful.

In my experience, they will call and question every move when you don't get results in the first week, and it's not because your service doesn't work or you need to do something differently.

It's usually because:

- They know they can't afford your service
- They don't know how to grow a business
- They would rather talk on the phone than hustle

So do yourself a favor and avoid these businesses.

SEO is a long-term game, and it should supplement a company's other forms of marketing. Not be the very first, do-or-die attempt at growing a business.

Productivity Lessons

11. Don't Let Email Control You

Hi, my name's Nathan. And I am a recovering email inbox addict who used to have Gmail open in a tab all day and compulsively check it countless times.

Sound familiar?

I only learned how much of a productivity killer this can be, thanks to the infamous entrepreneur Tim Ferris. So, I changed my habits and now only check my email twice daily.

Doing so has had a dramatic effect on my business and it's remarkably liberating. It has given me the confidence that I'm in control, not the people emailing me.

I decide when to respond. I decide how much time to spend on my emails. And most importantly, I eliminated the feeling of anxiety and stopped rationalizing why I needed to read each and every email right away.

My thoughts used to be:

"O-M-G... I wonder if (client name) has emailed me. I better check.

I wonder if I have a new lead.

That vendor said he would finish today. Let me check."

Here's the point: Stay out of your inbox. Set a clear boundary of how often you will open your inbox daily. To avoid getting trapped, I recommend you use an app like "Inbox Pause" and learn to batch your emails by responding to several at a time and even scheduling them to be sent out later to avoid responding too soon.

12. Create Systems & Processes
Your agency will live in chaos if you don't have clear

procedures and systems in place. At a bare minimum, you need to have clear processes for the following:

- Lead generation
- Sales
- Service fulfillment
- Client retention

Most service-based businesses have several moving parts that can be difficult to keep track of. Systems will bring clarity and end the chaos. Consider using templates and software solutions to make things easier.

For example, I use Google Drive, custom SOPs (standard operating procedures), and Asana to run my agency. By the way, I share all my SEO templates and current SOPs with members of Gotch SEO Academy (visit gotchseo.com to learn more).

Just remember: Always try to keep things simple, or your business (and your sanity) will suffer the consequences.

13. Avoid Decision Fatigue (At All Costs)

Decision fatigue occurs when you constantly have to think about "what to do next." Every decision you make throughout the day expends precious mental energy and affects your decision-making ability.

Why do you think Albert Einstein and Steve Jobs basically wore the same outfit every day? To quote Einstein, *"So that I don't waste any brainpower in the mornings deciding which set of clothes to wear."*

Now, you don't have to take it that far, but Mr. Einstein and Mr. Jobs obviously knew the limitations of their decision-making gas tanks. So other than your wardrobe, how do you solve the problem of decision fatigue?

First, limit how many decisions you're making on a daily basis by planning out your day in advance and focusing on a max of one or two important tasks. Once again, keep it simple and know that most tasks almost always take longer than expected.

It took me years to learn this lesson but now that I plan out my days ahead of time (Asana or Google Calendar is a must) and usually only work on one critical project per day, I can make much faster progress overall and save my decision-making fuel for key business decisions that move the needle.

14. Live and Die by 80/20

Now that I have employees, I can spend 80% of my time trying to grow my business instead of working in my business. For example, when I was a solopreneur, I used to spend 80% of my time fulfilling the work.

There's nothing wrong with that in the beginning, but I can now act as CEO, which requires a different mindset than being a freelancer. First, you must train and educate your team. But the most crucial part is to teach them how to get your clients great results without you.

I love using VAs, but nothing beats having full-time employees you can speak with virtually or in person. As you may recall , I was a college baseball player, so I love having a team atmosphere even though all my employees work from home.

The main lesson is you need to get to the point where you spend 80% of your time trying to grow your business. Don't worry if you are on the wrong side of this equation right now. It doesn't mean you can't start planning to flip to a growth equation slowly but surely.

Here's what you can do to start making the transition:

Every week you should examine how much time you are spending on clients. Then compare that to "growth-based" activities such as marketing, prospecting, and making offers on sales calls.

Begin the process of flipping the equation. Try changing the equation by 1% each week. For example, you may be 80/20 for service fulfillment/growth right now.

Next week, you should try 79% client fulfillment and 21% growth. That could simply mean send one follow-up email to a prospective client or ask a current client for a referral.

At this rate, you will be at 68/32 within a year. Therefore, 68% of your time will focus on growth and 32% on client fulfillment. You get the point.

Changing your mindset from scarcity to growth is beyond powerful. You begin to act like a CEO. You stop worrying about whether a client is going to leave you or not. Your business grows because you stop spending most of your time on maintenance tasks.

It all boils down to this: Stop being an employee and start being a CEO.

15. Leverage VAs

To achieve the target of 80/20, you will have to use VAs or hire an employee. Unless you want to feel like an employee for the rest of your life, you can't do it all alone. And who would want to, anyway? I don't think that's the goal for 99.9% of self-employed individuals.

Let's face it, you started your own business because you want to be in control. You left the nine-to-five because you don't want to be an employee! Well guess what? You now have the opportunity to truly break free. But you need to be willing to delegate tasks.

There are only so many hours in a day, and you must cherish every minute. Here's the good news: You can delegate almost every task in your SEO business one way or another.

Lessons Clients Have Taught Me

16. Your Client's Success Is Your Success

News flash: Clients want results! If they are successful, chances are your business will be successful as well. However, the opposite is also true. If most of your clients are not successful, make no mistake; it will bring your business down.

Social proof means everything these days and it doesn't take many online reviews to make your business sink or swim.

So before you start taking clients in any industry, ensure you clearly understand how to – and are fully committed to – get amazing, mind-blowing results.

Remember what I said earlier? Practice what you preach. And skill up before you scale up.

17. Some Clients Will NEVER Be Happy

Look, in business and in life, there are good seeds and bad seeds.

It doesn't matter how likable you are, there will always be a small percentage of clients who you will never please. Right from the beginning, they will critique every tiny detail of your work.

They will complain about communication even though you spend more time with them than any other client. They will also complain weekly, sometimes daily, about the results. Then, once you get them results, they will complain about not being number one for every single keyword.

Sounds fun, right?

These types of clients will make you lose sleep at night. But only if you let them.

I'm extreme and will straight up fire clients who are time-sucks and unreasonable.

Realize one unfortunate thing: No matter how good your discovery/vetting phase is, you will end up with a bad client from time to time. All you can do is have a strong discovery phase to avoid it becoming a regular occurrence. And most importantly, trust your gut.

Like my business partner Simon always says, *"how it starts is how it ends."* And if the client is a major pain in the you-know-what from day one, it never gets better in my experience. Only more of the same headaches down the road.

So do yourself a favor and respectfully cut ties with them as soon as possible. A short 'n sweet email containing "I don't think we're a good fit" is a favorite of mine.

18. Your Most Unreasonable Clients Will Be Your Cheapest Clients

I'm speaking for my business and in general. In my experience, my worst clients are almost always my lowest paying clients.

But don't get it twisted. There's nothing wrong with charging lower monthly retainers when you're just starting out. And I've had plenty of terrific clients who are on my lowest payment tier.

The clients I'm referring to are the ones who make it clear that price is the only factor that concerns them. Sometimes these clients will ask for your pricing right away on a sales call. Others will ironically tell you that "the money doesn't matter" when you present your offer which explains the old sales adage, "buyers are liars."

Another red flag is a complete lack of questions or interest during your sales presentation, since they don't see the value in what you do as an SEO professional. It's also not uncommon for them to haggle or try negotiating special lower rates.

Just remember that price is relative. Someone paying $500 a month may think that's a colossal amount. And they may also think they deserve the world. They don't.

In reality, we know that $500 a month is pennies for a real SEO campaign. So be wary of cheap clients who think they're entitled to more than they can afford. They're not.

19. Always Have A Contract

Contracts or SOWs (statements of work) are important for both parties to clearly outline the terms of your agreement. They should include everything from project scopes, objectives, and deliverables, to payment terms and legal disclaimers. However, if a prospect doesn't want to sign a contract? Run for the hills.

Trust me on this. A prospect who won't sign some form of written agreement will be a problem. Every. Single. Time.

And you will end up kicking yourself (like I have in the past), asking, "Why didn't I just have this person sign a contract?" So be smart; use contracts.

20. Set Clear Boundaries with Clients

At the onset, it's super important to set clear boundaries for your business and working relationships. For example, what are your agency's hours of operation? How often are you going to be updating and speaking with clients? How much communication will be virtual or over the phone versus email? How do you measure and report progress?

Know the answers to these questions and establish crystal clear boundaries early on.

Otherwise, you will have clients contact you and expect replies at all hours of the day and night – like the time a client texted me at 11:00 pm. This will not only make you miserable but will greatly disrupt your team's workflow and hurt productivity.

Remember: As much as some clients would like to believe, they don't own you.

21. Fire Clients Who Don't Pay on Time

Let's say your invoice goes out on the first of the month. Then days, weeks, and sometimes a month goes by with no payment. And even though you haven't been paid, the client believes you should still be working.

That's fair, right? Believe it or not, it happens more than you'd expect.

Imagine going into a traditional nine-to-five job, and your boss announces that he can't pay you for thirty days. Of course, he might pay you within thirty days, or the delay could even extend to forty-five days.

That's cool, right?

No, you'd probably raise hell. So would I. So would your client who hasn't paid their invoice yet. But for some strange reason, the normal rules don't apply to them because they're special.

Please listen to this advice: Clients who don't pay on time will never pay on time. So, don't waste your breath and struggle to keep clients like this.

They are disrespectful, selfish, and chasing money like a debt collector is incredibly frustrating and exhausting. Fire them because many clients will pay on time.

22. Beware of Accepting PayPal

Unfortunately, we've all heard of shady SEO companies that take advantage of unsuspecting business owners and give our industry a bad name.

But how many times have you heard about a business owner screwing over the SEO company?

It's happened to my agency on a couple of occasions.

Here's how it usually goes down:

In the beginning, everything's cool, and the client hires you but requests to pay via PayPal. You do everything you said you would do, and BOOM, after a month, all of a sudden they open a PayPal dispute for no reason and ghost you.

So what happened?

Well, since you've already done all the heavy lifting for the first month, the client is opening a PayPal dispute to try and get your service for free.

The good news?

As long as you've actually done the agreed-upon work, you should win the PayPal dispute – I did. Yet another reason why you always need a signed contract in place. Better yet, avoid the drama completely by not accepting payments through PayPal – I don't anymore.

23. Never Negotiate on Price

I made this rookie mistake for well over a year when I first started out. I would send off a proposal with only one price option and hope the client would accept it. While this worked a lot, it also cost me several thousand dollars in missed contracts.

That's when I discovered that I needed to have three pricing options.

Duh, right?

When you only have one pricing option, the client must take it or leave it and choose "Yes" or "No." But when you have three options, it moves them from "take it or leave it" to "which option is best for me?"

This is a well-known and proven method for increasing sales since it incorporates psychology (lets them choose a price) and by offering a wider payment range (low, medium, high), you'll increase the chance of meeting what the client is willing to pay.

Sure, they can still say no, but it decreases the likelihood.

24. Stop Saying "Yes" To Everyone

I'm not sure how to say this but I'm kind of a big deal. People know me. Kidding. But seriously, I get a lot of leads. And I say no to 99% of them. At this stage in my business, I can pretty much tell who can and cannot afford my services. I also have very high standards for who I choose to work with.

As previously mentioned, I won't work with startups. But I also won't work with any business in niches that I'm not comfortable with such as gambling, escorts, porn, or anything illegal.

It's a personal choice but I'd prefer not to associate myself with such businesses. That's why I say no. But, of course, I also say no to cheapskates or rude clients who I just don't vibe with for one reason or another.

That said, I'm in a fortunate position that you may not be in if you're just beginning your SEO journey and are struggling to find leads to talk to.

If that's the case, you may need to eat some dirt before you get to the carrot, so to speak. But never compromise your integrity just to get a deal.

The lure of "easy money" can lead you into bad situations.

So trust your gut. If a client is giving you major red flags, don't be afraid to say "No" and walk away. There will always be another opportunity around the corner.

25. Fulfillment Is Hard

Every results-based business struggles with one thing:

Getting excellent results 100% of the time.

I'm willing to bet there isn't a single SEO agency with more than thirty clients that hasn't found it extremely challenging to get results at least once. It doesn't matter how good you are.

There's been plenty of times I've struggled to get amazing results for my clients. And it's not because my strategy doesn't work or because I don't know what I'm doing.

In most cases, it's because I didn't screen the client well enough. I ignored obvious red flags in the discovery phase because I was chasing the money.

Here are the two biggest mistakes I've made with clients regarding results:

+ Underestimating how long it would take to rank
+ Underquoting how much it would cost to rank

The combination of these two errors leads to massive frustration on both sides.

To avoid both situations, ensure you screen each client down to the last detail. Do not sign up any client until you know with absolute certainty that A) you can deliver the results they're looking for in a realistic timeframe and B) they are paying enough to get excellent results.

This is why it's so important to set realistic expectations during your sales calls.

For example, I typically aim to see solid ranking movement within the first 2-3 months of a campaign for most of my client's primary keywords. But when I do a preliminary audit of their site, I'll also get a rough estimate of how much content and backlinks they'll need to achieve those targets.

Armed with this information, it helps to identify near-impossible, no-win situations up front such as a client with a brand new website who's trying to quickly rank for keywords with a KD of 80+ against websites who have hundreds of thousands of backlinks.

It's not gonna happen. So be honest with clients who need a reality check and once again, don't chase the money because it will always end up hurting you in the long run.

Basic Business Lessons

*Disclaimer: I'm not a tax, law, or financial advisor. Everything I'm discussing in this section is from personal experience. Always consult with an expert before making any financial or tax-related decisions.

26. Take A Profit-First Approach

Straight talk: What's the point of owning a business if you aren't making a profit?

The cold, hard reality is at least 50% of businesses fail within the first 5 years and the number one reason is lack of capital or funding, i.e. they're not profitable.

If you're anything like me, you probably started your business to escape the nine-to-five and be your own boss. But that freedom requires you to earn more than you spend, so you need to structure your service and fulfillment to turn a profit.

Now obviously, if you're just starting out and have little to no clients yet, you might not be profitable right out of the gate. It's no secret that businesses are expensive to launch and operate – welcome to the wonderful world of being an entrepreneur.

However, once you're up and running, you must develop sound financial habits such as having actual profit targets, always taking profits first, and paying your bills last.

I highly recommend reading the book "Profit First" by Michael Michalowicz. It changed the way I run my business and I've never been more profitable after following his advice.

27. Learn About Taxes and Hire A Good Accountant

If you don't understand taxes, you will get destroyed. I'm speaking from experience here.

For example, I didn't adjust my quarterly tax estimates in my first full year of business even though my business was much larger than the previous year.

Guess what happened?

I ended up owing $25,000 in taxes and contributed $36,000 to my solo 401(k) to avoid more tax burden. The worst part is that I had to come up with that amount of cash in a small amount of time.

It sucked beyond measure, and I vowed to never let it happen again.

The following year, I changed my LLC's tax status to an "S-Corp."

I also made sure to contribute to my retirement account monthly to avoid giving up one lump sum of cash.

Why am I telling you this?

Because I don't want you to make the same mistakes! Learn about taxes and talk to a highly-rated CPA.

28. Structure Your Business Right

As I explained above, I started my business as an LLC but got taxed as a sole proprietor. And I got killed on taxes because of this.

To this day, my business is still an LLC but is taxed as an S-Corp.

In essence, I pay myself a reasonable salary as an employee. Then, after I've paid myself a reasonable salary, I can take distributions (profit) from the business.

For those doing business in the USA, here's why an S-Corp is awesome:

- My salary is tax-deductible

- I don't have to pay self-employment or payroll taxes on distributions (profit)

- Contributions to an SEP IRA are a tax deduction for the business

No matter what country you're doing business in, research and find out if your current business structure is benefiting you. Once again, this is where an excellent CPA can help tremendously.

29. Diversify Your Income Streams

If one hundred percent of your business revenue comes from one source or client, you need to sit down and think about that. What if that one revenue source disappeared tomorrow, and you had no income?

That's a loaded question, but you get the point. One is the most dangerous number in business. Ideally, you need to have several income streams to protect your business against worst-case scenarios.

Trust me, having more than one source of revenue gives you incredible leverage. Not only does it provide a safety blanket, but it can boost your confidence so you don't have to play the price game with clients.

You can decide how much you're worth and what clients you want. Most importantly, you'll stop chasing money.

If you run a service-based business, there are many options for you to explore. For example, in addition to the client side of Gotch SEO, we offer SEO training through Gotch SEO Academy. I also own affiliate sites.

The point is one revenue source ties you down. So, think long and hard about how you can diversify your revenue. At the very least, aim to build a solid portfolio of clients so that if a few leave in the same month, you won't get wiped out.

30. Invest in Yourself

As cliche as it sounds, you have to be willing to invest in yourself.

It's crazy to think how I've become such an avid reader and learner because I was such a horrible student in school.

But now I can't learn enough.

Here's a simple idea that changed my life: To make more money, you have to become more valuable. If you want more, you have to become more.

You must obsess about learning and developing new skills to increase your value to the marketplace. Skills pay the bills. Like the late, great Jim Rohn said, "Learn to work harder on yourself than you do on your job. Formal education will make you a living. But self-education will make you a fortune."

So don't be afraid to invest in yourself. Buy and read business books, take courses, go to conferences, do whatever it takes to win.

To quote another mentor of mine, the marketing genius Dan Kennedy, *"You don't get free, rich, or secure by what you do. You get it by what you own. The hardest asset to lose is YOU. Your mindset, personality, and skillset."*

And since you invested in this book and reached the end, you're ahead of the game.

But don't stop there.

Consider joining us in Gotch SEO Academy: gotchseo.com/academy/

Acknowledgements

Any level of success I've achieved is because of other people who have graciously helped me throughout my journey. It takes a village, and you can't be a successful entrepreneur without help. And that's why I want to thank the following people:

Gramps

"Gramps" (my grandpa) was the fatherly figure in my life when my parents split when I was young. Thank you for teaching me the value of hard work and how to be selfless.

My Wife

No one believed in me more than her when I decided to commit to entrepreneurship. She was there every single step of the way. Even when I was making pennies doing paid surveys. There's never been a single second that she hasn't supported me. I love you!

My Children

Thank you, Kinsie and Nolan, for humbling me and showing me what it means to be a kid again. Everything I do is for you guys. I love you so incredibly much.

My Family

Thank you to everyone who supports me: Mom, Dad, Laura, Kathleen, Keevin, Heather, Alyssa, and Wes.

Coach Paciorek

Coach Paciorek was a one-of-a-kind baseball coach, but his lasting impact on me is based on who he is. He didn't need to lecture us about how to be a good, contributing person to society. He demonstrated what that looks like through his actions. Coach Paciorek taught me what it means to have integrity and the importance of giving back to the community.

My Mentors

Thank you to the following people for supporting me and teaching me so much (even if I haven't told you): Simon L. Smith, Rob Timmermann, Chris Dreyer, and so many others.

References

Globe Newswire. (2022). *Search Engine Optimization Services market is expected to reach $134.26 billion in 2026 at a CAGR of 20.7%.* https://www.globenewswire.com/en/news-release/2022/05/06/2437534/0/en/Search-Engine-Optimization-Services-market-is-expected-to-reach-134-26-billion-in-2026-at-a-CAGR-of-20-7.html

Forbes. (2022). *5 Industries Experiencing Double-Digit Growth Over The Next Decade.* https://www.forbes.com/sites/ashleystahl/2022/04/08/5-industries-experiencing-double-digit-growth-over-the-next-decade/

Ahrefs. (2018). *SEO Pricing: ~350 Agencies, Consultants, and Freelancers Reveal How Much SEO Costs.* https://ahrefs.com/blog/seo-pricing/

Search Engine Journal. (2022). *Could 57% Of North American SMBs Still Lack An SEO Strategy?* https://www.searchenginejournal.com/no-seo-strategy-2022/438639/

Backlinko. (2022). *The SEO Services Report.* https://backlinko.com/seo-services-statistics

Ahrefs. (2020). *90.63% of Content Gets No Traffic From Google. And How to Be in the Other 9.37% [New Research for 2020].* https://ahrefs.com/blog/search-traffic-study/

Harvard (2015). *Increase the Odds of Achieving Your Goals by Setting Them with Your Spouse.* https://hbr.org/2015/02/increase-the-odds-of-achieving-your-goals-by-setting-them-with-your-spouse

Tim Ferriss on Goal Setting: Rig the Game So You Can Win it. (2016). [Video]. YouTube. https://youtu.be/fwjZ99aNsa4

AFCPE (2018). *The Power of Accountability.* https://www.afcpe.org/news-and-publications/the-standard/2018-3/the-power-of-accountability/

Inc (2022). *A New Study Shows 1 in 5 Successful Entrepreneurs Use Vision Boards.* The Results Are Backed by Neuroscience. https://www.inc.com/marla-tabaka/study-shows-1-in-5-successful-entrepreneurs-use-vision-boards-backed-by-neuroscience.html

Clutch (2022). *40 Best SEO Companies & Services.* https://clutch.co/seo-firms

Wikipedia (2022). *List of companies named after people.* https://en.wikipedia.org/wiki/List_of_companies_named_after_people

Zippia (2022). *Ogilvy Revenue: Annual, Historic, And Financials.* https://www.zippia.com/ogilvy-careers-33543/revenue/

Statista (2019). *Number of professionally active dentists working in the U.S.* https://www.statista.com/statistics/1114666/number-of-active-dentists-by-practice-area-us/

Cloudflare (2022). *How website performance affects conversion rates.* https://www.cloudflare.com/learning/performance/more/website-performance-conversion-rates/

Harvard (2022). *How Selfish Are People—Really?* https://hbr.org/1989/05/how-selfish-are-people-really

City Headshots (2022). *How Much Do Headshots Cost in 2022?* https://www.cityheadshots.com/typical-pricing.html

JAMA Netw Open (2021). *Public Perceptions of Physician Attire and Professionalism in the US.* https://jamanetwork.com/journals/jamanetworkopen/fullarticle/2782564

Upwork (2022). *[Screenshot of of Upwork Profile Page].* https://www.upwork.com/freelancers/~010b1d551b48cad03f

Ahrefs. (2020). *90.63% of Content Gets No Traffic From Google. And How to Be in the Other 9.37% [New Research for 2020].* https://ahrefs.com/blog/search-traffic-study/

Better Proposals. (2016). *The Ultimate Guide to Following-Up After Sending a Proposal.* https://betterproposals.io/blog/the-ultimate-guide-to-following-up-after-sending-a-proposal/

Backlinko. (2022). *We Analyzed 4 Million Google Search Results. Here's What We Learned About Organic CTR.* https://backlinko.com/google-ctr-stats

Stanford. (2016). *The Google PageRank Algorithm.* https://web.stanford.edu/class/cs54n/handouts/24-GooglePageRankAlgorithm.pdf

English Google SEO office-hours from February 19, 2021. (2021). [Video]. YouTube. https://youtu.be/zCV6tEt3w0k

Psychology Today. (2022). *Heuristics.* https://www.psychologytoday.com/us/basics/heuristics

Backlinko. (2022). *We Analyzed 912 Million Blog Posts. Here's What We Learned About Content Marketing.* https://backlinko.com/content-study

Made in the USA
Monee, IL
07 August 2024

63375856R10193